FULFORD SCHOOL
FULFORDGATE
HESLINGTON LANE
FULFORD   YORK
YO10 4FY

Fulford School
Mathematics & Computing College
Resource Centre

Tel: 01904 633300

EXPLORING
NORTH YORKSHIRE'S
HISTORY

EXPLORING
NORTH YORKSHIRE'S
HISTORY

NIGEL A. IBBOTSON

breedon **books**
PUBLISHING

First published in Great Britain in 2009 by

The Breedon Books Publishing Company Limited

Breedon House, 3 The Parker Centre, Derby, DE21 4SZ.

ISBN 978-1-85983-723-8

Printed and bound by MKT Print, Slovenia

CONTENTS

INTRODUCTION

The magnificent county of North Yorkshire is the largest in England; it is almost 100 miles wide and 65 miles long, and covers an area of over 3,000 square miles. It is a county of astonishing diversity and one which offers the visitor an unparalleled variety of scenery; from cragged hills, numerous valleys through which fast running rivers meander and moorlands with thick blankets of dense heather, to fields of rich arable land and rugged coastline. It boasts two National Parks: the Yorkshire Dales and the North Yorkshire Moors, which attract hundreds of thousands of visitors each year and together account for 40 per cent of the county. But it would be a mistake to imagine that, breathtaking as it is, this picture postcard county has only its stupendous views to offer, for the region is also rich in history and has played its part to the fullest in the affairs of this great kingdom.

North Yorkshire has been the birthplace of princes, kings and even a Roman emperor. It has not only been admired by rulers, but has also been fought over by those wishing to rule. It has produced great thinkers, writers, artists, scientists and revolutionaries, men and women who have lived and sometimes died by their principles, sometimes in deaths that were unthinkably cruel. The pages of its history are not only filled with the deeds of the famous and the infamous, but also by the humble folk who have eked out their existence in the cities, towns, villages and hamlets which make up this great county. They are the unsung heroes who have played their part in creating the story of North Yorkshire: the sheep farmers, the lead miners, the fishermen and the smugglers, to name but a few.

The land has been soaked with the blood of thousands of combatants and the rivers have run red, for the county has been the location of many a battle. It was the scene of the bloodiest battle ever to be fought on British soil, and one which is reputed to have taken more lives than the first day of the Battle of the Somme. The largest battle of the English Civil War was also fought here. It has been the battleground for many a skirmish between the English and the Scottish. In 1069 it felt the heavy hand of William the Conqueror's reprisals when he heaped his anger upon the people of the North and left the land barren and waste in the 'Harrying of the North'. The wrath and indignation caused by this monstrous crime reverberated through the centuries, and we are reminded that some things run too deep to ever be forgotten.

Our journey begins in the beautiful city of York. This ancient place was once briefly the centre of the Roman Empire and centuries later would almost become the capital of England: had it not been for the deposing of a king, the historic landscape of this country might have been markedly different. It is truly a wonderful city, in which every stone and every brick is steeped in history, with stupendous buildings such as York Minster, the Guildhall and the stunning timber-framed Merchant Adventurers' Hall. But the history of this fabulous city is more than its bricks and mortar, more than its monuments and great buildings; it is also the history of the people who inhabited its streets and buildings.

North Yorkshire is unarguably a county of unrivalled beauty, and one which truly deserves the title of 'God's own county'. But it is also a place which is rightly proud of its heritage, for it has been the backdrop to many of the events which have shaped this country. This book invites the reader to explore this exciting county with a combination of contemporary colour photographs and text. We shall examine some of the well-known historical sites, as well as some of those which are perhaps lesser known, and our journey will take us from the grand to the more whimsical events that have shaped this land.

Nigel A. Ibbotson
May 2009

ACKNOWLEDGEMENTS

I wish first to express my heartfelt gratitude to Kathryn, without whose support and encouragement this book would not have been possible. She has never once complained at the early morning starts which were necessary to obtain the best light for the photographs. She even kept her humour when we were stuck in snow during a homeward journey and with every prospect of being stranded for the foreseeable future, for the police had informed us that all the roads were blocked. We were just considering our next move in a seemingly hopeless situation when the fortuitous arrival of a snowplough allowed us the opportunity to continue on our journey.

I also wish to thank my father Mr A.L. Ibbotson, who was born and brought up in Scarborough, for spending the time showing me many of the town's points of historical interest. I should also like to acknowledge my indebtedness to Mr Ernest Spacey for his diligent reading and correcting of my drafts, and for the suggestions which have greatly improved the final result.

While collecting the material for this volume I have had the privilege of meeting many kind people, who have greatly assisted me in this project. I should like to take this opportunity to sincerely apologise for any inadvertent errors or omissions, and I wish to express my gratitude to the following people: Mr Mark Thompson for allowing me to photograph Hardraw Force and Nappa Hall; Dawn Webster, the curator of Kiplin Hall, for allowing me to photograph the wonderful Jacobean country house; Lt Col Ian Horsford for allowing me to photograph the magnificent Ripon Cathedral; Father Antony Pritchett of St Peter and St Paul's Church in Pickering; and the Reverend Barry Pyke of St Oswald's Church, Lythe. I am also indebted to the Earl of Ronaldshay for taking time out of his busy schedule to meet me and for his kind permission to allow me the opportunity to photograph Aske Hall.

I also wish to say thank you to Steve Caron, Michelle Harrison and the team at Breedon Books.

THE CITY OF YORK

George VI once said that the history of the ancient city of York is the history of England, and there can be no denying that this stunning city is rich in history and has witnessed many pivotal moments in the story of this magnificent realm. During the Scottish Wars (1298–1337) the English government was moved to York by Edward I, where it remained for seven years until he sent it back to Westminster in 1307. So great has been its attraction that in the 14th century Richard II wanted to make it the capital of England, and had he not been deposed before he had fulfilled his plans, the historical landscape of this country might have been profoundly different.

As a result of the Local Government Act of 1972, the county of North Yorkshire was formed in 1974. It included most of the lands of the historic North Riding, part of the West Riding, a good portion of the East Riding and what was formerly the county borough of York. In 1996, however, York became a unitary authority, which meant that although it was independent from North Yorkshire County Council, it still formed part of the ceremonial county for a number of functions, such as those which require the attendance of the Lord Lieutenant of North Yorkshire.

EBORACUM – ROMAN YORK

In AD71 the Romans, under Quintus Petillius Cerialis, who was the Roman Governor of Britain, established Eboracum. Initially it had been a camp for the Ninth Legion, who had been sent to subdue the warring Brigantes in the North. It was chosen because of its ideal location, being situated at the junction of the rivers Ouse and Foss. It was soon, however, to become a permanent fortress. It was Ptolemy who in AD150 was to first record the place as Eborakon, which possibly meant 'a place of yew-trees'. Its name later became Latinised as Eboracum, and when the Anglo-Saxons settled in the area they anglicised the name to Eoforwic (meaning 'wild boar town').

During his northern campaigns Hadrian had chosen this site as his headquarters. Interestingly, he was responsible for establishing the female figure of Britannia as the personification of Britain, when he had a shrine erected at York to Britain as a goddess and called her Britannia. He also had coins struck which portrayed her image. It was from York that the Emperor Septimus Severus ruled the Roman Empire for two years until his untimely death from an illness on 4 February AD211. The city was also the place where the Emperor Flavius Valerius Constantius died in AD306. Better known as Chorus, he was the father of

*Opposite:
York's famous
Shambles was once
a street of butchers.
Its name is derived
from 'Shammel'
benches, which
were once used to
display meat.*

*Standing near to
the Minster is a
Roman column,
which once stood
within the Great
Hall of the Sixth
Legion's
Headquarters. It
was found during
excavations of the
Minster's south
transept in 1969,
and was lying
where it had
originally
collapsed.*

A detail of the statue of Constantine: he was proclaimed emperor near to this spot.

Also near the Minster stands the statue of the Roman Emperor Constantine the Great (274–337), who was the first Christian Emperor and founder of Constantinople. He was responsible for establishing the religious foundations of Western Christendom.

Constantine the Great (the first Christian emperor) and consequently a number of Christian legends have developed around him. In AD306 Constantine was proclaimed Roman emperor while in York, and a statue of him stands near the spot where this took place. It is therefore clear that even from the earliest days of this magnificent city its great importance was recognised.

There is a current trend of thought which believes that Constantine was not actually a Christian, but tolerated what at this time was just a small cult. In AD314, however, he invited three British bishops to attend the Council of Arles, where they discussed doctrinal matters. These three bishops were 'Eborus, Episcopus de Civitate Eboracensi; Restitutus, Episcopus de Civitate Londinensi; Adelfius, Episcopus de Col. Londinensium' (possibly Lincoln). As these bishops were mentioned in order of precedence, it is easy to appreciate the importance of York. In AD407 the Romans withdrew from Britain, but even today the Archbishop of York still signs himself 'Ebor', so we are reminded of their influence.

The earliest written reference to York dates from about AD100 and was found on a wooden tablet unearthed at Vindolanda, the famous fort near Hadrian's Wall. Life in Roman York would have been on the whole quite prosperous and peaceful, at least until nearly the end of the fourth century. The fifth century, however, brought a rapid deterioration in its fortunes, and by the second decade York (as well as the rest of Britain) was no longer part of the Roman

Empire. With the departure of the Romans, York was thrown into what is known as the Dark Ages.

EOFERWIC – ANGLO-SAXON YORK

After the Romans had left, Saxon settlers began to arrive in the area and were soon established in York, which they called Eoforwic. It is difficult to put together a clear picture of how the settlement would have been during this period for the early Saxons left few written records, and of those that they did leave many were destroyed by the Vikings, while those that survived untouched were extirpated by the Normans. In addition, very little archaeological evidence from the period has been unearthed.

According to legend, King Arthur briefly won back York from the Saxon invaders. In AD625 St Paulinus established the diocese of York. He had been sent by Pope Gregory the Great to assist St Augustine with his missionary work in Britain. It was while undertaking this work that he accompanied the daughter of King Aethlbert of Kent as her chaplain; she married the pagan Northumbrian King Edwin and St Paulinus made the most of the opportunity by converting the king.

ALCUIN (735–804)

Alcuin was born in AD735 to well-to-do parents and was sent to York to study, for by the eighth century the city had become a famous centre for learning. It was here that he was taught by the renowned Ecgberht, who had himself been a disciple of the Venerable Bede. Ecgberht was brother to Eadbert, who at that time was King of Northumbria, and together they were instrumental in reorganising and revitalising the English church. In AD757 Eadbert abdicated and spent his remaining years as a monk at York, leaving the throne to his son Oswulf.

This was a golden age for learning and York had not only become a centre for religious studies, but also the liberal arts, literature and the sciences. After completing his studies at St Peter's School in York, Alcuin remained there as a teacher. The school is one of the oldest in the United Kingdom, having been established by St Paulinus in AD627. It was in about AD767 that Alcuin became head of the school.

In AD781 Alcuin was sent to Rome by King Elfwald to petition the Pope for an official confirmation of York's status as an archbishopric and also to confirm the election of a new archbishop. It was during his journey home that he met Charlemagne (Charles the Great). Although a successful warrior, who had created the Frankish Empire, Charlemagne was extremely interested in scholarship, so much so that he created a centre for learning. He had invited many of the greatest minds of the age to work for him. Charlemagne made Alcuin an offer which created a dilemma for the scholar: a choice between returning to his beloved school in York or working for the Emperor. Ultimately, it was impossible for him to refuse, as his love of the church and his intellectual curiosity proved too great. Alcuin was soon installed at the Palace School of Charlemagne among an illustrious group of scholars, which included great names such as Peter of Pisa, Paulinus of Aquileia, Rado and Abbot Fulrad. He was appointed head of this school in Aachen and it was here that he developed the Carolingian minuscule, which was to become the basis of how we write the Roman alphabet today. He was also responsible for the priceless Carolingian codices, also known as the *Golden Gospels*: a series of manuscripts which were written in gold on purple vellum. It was the development of this script that would play a large part in the history of mathematics. The advantage of this script over the previous unspaced capital script was that it was clear to read. During the ninth century the majority of the work of the ancient Greek mathematicians was copied out into Carolingian minuscule and has consequently been preserved for posterity.

When Alcuin retired from the Palace School in AD796, he took the post of abbot at the Abbey of St Martin's at Tours, France. While there, he had his monks continue with his script and he arranged for a number of his pupils to travel to York to retrieve some of the rarer works that he had collected. During his life he wrote numerous texts on arithmetic, geometry and astronomy, and he was also instrumental in starting a renaissance of learning in Europe. Alcuin summed up his career as follows: 'In the morning, at the height of my powers, I sowed my seed in Britain, now in the evening when my blood is growing cold I am still sowing in France, hoping both will grow, by the grace of God, giving some the honey of the Holy Scriptures, making others drunk on the old wine of ancient learning...'

He died on 19 May AD804; his life dedicated to learning and his love of the church. Strangely, he was never ordained as a priest, and, although he lived his life as a monk, officially he never was one. He was a brave man who spoke his mind and on at least one occasion this candour brought him into conflict with Charlemagne. At the time it had been the emperor's policy to force pagans either to be baptised, or to face the death penalty: Alcuin argued that faith is a free act of will and should not be forced, as no one can be made to believe. This point of view was very progressive for its time and would take many generations to be generally accepted. His arguments, however, prevailed and the death penalty for paganism was abolished.

Vox Populi, Vox Dei

The voice of the people is the voice of God

(Alcuin 735–804)

JORVIK – VIKING YORK

By the middle of the ninth century Viking raids were becoming increasingly intensive and well organised. Civil war in Northumbria had greatly weakened the region and the Vikings were quick to take advantage. On 1 November 866 Ivar the Boneless captured York, but it was his half-brother, Halfdan Ragnarsson, who was to found Jorvik. Using the still-strong Roman walls of the old city as a foundation, they built a fortress. The Viking rulers built their palace in an area of York that is now called King's Square: they called it Konungsgårthr. The following year the Saxon kings Aella and Osbert, who had previously been enemies, combined their forces in an attempt to drive their common foe out of the city. Osbert was to die in the storming of the defences and Aella was captured by the Vikings. He was cruelly tortured to death and an eagle was ritually carved into his back. The Viking hold of York was now secure and would be so for nearly 100 years. In 954 the Viking kingdom of Jorvik became absorbed into England (although it was to retain some independence, which would end with the arrival of William the Conqueror).

ERIC BLOODAXE

Perhaps one of the most renowned Vikings to have ruled Jorvik was Eric Bloodaxe or *Eiríkr blóðøx* (Old Norse). Born in around 895 in Norway, he was the eldest son of Harald Fairhair, who was reputed to be the first king of Norway. It is said that Harald fathered around 20 sons. Although credited with the unification of Norway, in reality his kingdom was much more limited and would have only included the west and south-west of the country. This limited kingdom would not support the aspirations of his 20 sons and Eric (thought to be the eldest) made sure that he secured his inheritance by systematically murdering his brothers. It was from these acts of fratricide that Eric would gain his nickname 'Bloodaxe' and not, as commonly imagined, from any prowess in battle: certain Latin chronicles referred to him as *fratis interfector* (brother killer).

In 930 Eric became the second king of Norway, but his reign was short-lived and lasted only four harsh years. He was a cruel and unpopular king, and when his rule was challenged by his only surviving brother, Hakon, the people of Norway readily accepted his sibling as their new sovereign. Hakon had been brought up in the court of the English king Athelstan, which had presumably saved him from the same fate as his other brothers. Returning from England, he laid claim to his inheritance in an apparently bloodless coup, for it appears Eric fled without a fight. Now in exile, the deposed king arrived on the shores of Northumbria, where he was warmly welcomed and accepted as their ruler by the Norsemen living there, who were delighted to be led by someone of royal descent from Norway.

It has been suggested that Eric had been invited to be king of Northumbria by Athelstan, who had wished to create a buffer zone against the warring Scots; this, however, is highly unlikely, as Eric became king of York and ruled Northumbria in 947, whereas Athelstan had died some eight years earlier. Eric's rule of Northumbria was by no means smooth and on a number of occasions he was driven out by rivals. Finally, he was killed in an ambush at Stainmore (once in Yorkshire but now Cumbria) in 954 by Maccus, son of Olaf Cuaran (king of Dublin). It appears that Olaf may have been one of Eric's rivals for kingship of Northumbria. With his death came the end of the rule of the Vikings at York.

THE BATTLE OF FULFORD

In 1066, while waiting for the anticipated arrival of William's invading army, King Harold was to receive grievous news of another invasion, which was taking place in the north of England. Three hundred ships containing an army of Norwegian Vikings had swept down the Yorkshire coast, dropping raiding parties at various points along their route. This force belonged to Harald Hardråde, king of Norway, who believed that he also had a claim to the throne of England. There were a number of English ships in the North Sea, but rather than engage the superior numbers of the Norwegian flotilla, they hastily withdrew and sailed firstly up the River Ouse and then up the Wharfe, where they took refuge at Tadcaster. While en route, Harald had joined up with his English ally Tostig, who was brother to the king of England. Tostig had been banished and in return for his treachery he had been offered his own English lands.

King Harold had been preoccupied by the threat of invasion from William, so when news came of the Norwegian army it would have come as a total shock to him, even though the north of the country would have been well aware of the advancing force. He now faced a

Germany Beck at Fulford, where the English army lined up their forces to face the Norwegian Harald Hardråde and his Viking army on 20 September 1066 at the Battle of Fulford.

serious crisis: an imminent invasion force in the south and the Viking army that had landed in the north. Fortune, however, was to smile on him, as a strong northerly wind kept William's troops landlocked on the other side of the Channel. This gave Harold the opportunity to march his army northwards to face the Norwegian threat. Although he marched with remarkable speed, he was unable to reach Yorkshire until his northern army had taken a beating at the hands of the invaders. This largely forgotten Battle of Fulford took place on 20 September 1066.

After the English ships had reached the safe haven of Tadcaster, it was not long before the Norwegians followed their route up the River Ouse, where they eventually landed at Riccall. The Norwegian king and his army of 8,000 warriors were now just 10 miles south of York, and, placing a number of guards with his ships, he marched his force towards the city. The English Earls Edwin and Morcar rallied their northern army to meet the advancing Vikings. It was the English that were to make the first strike against the invaders, making their attack before the Norwegians could fully deploy their forces. It was a bold move, but the English force were confident and soon Harald's troops were being forced back towards the marshlands. However, their initial success was short-lived and not enough to gain victory, and the Norwegians were able to bring fresh troops into the battle. Even though they were outnumbered, they slowly began to win ground from the battle-weary defenders. Eventually, the defenders were the ones outnumbered and outmanoeuvred, and before long they were forced to surrender.

The city of York now lay vulnerable and at the mercy of the invaders; however, rather than attack the city, it appears that Harald retreated to his ships, though not before he had taken the precaution of demanding hostages (and food).

Once he had returned to his ships he arranged a treaty. Although he never received his promised hostages, he was no doubt still in high spirits and, after his initial success, was feeling very confident. Perhaps he was too confident, for he was unprepared for what would happen five days later when he met with King Harold and his English army at Stamford Bridge.

THE ARRIVAL OF THE NORMANS

Following the death of King Harold on the battlefield of Hastings, William the Conqueror took the throne of England. But his conquest was far from over, for although he had vanquished England's only organised army, he was still faced with an uphill struggle. Even prior to the invasion, the country had been plagued by internal struggles. This disunity, which had proved so advantageous to his invasion, now became a major obstacle to his subjugation of the people. Even after two years the North of England remained defiant under the Saxon lords, Edwin and Morcar. In 1068 William gathered his army and marched north to put down the rebellion once and for all. This led to what has become known as the 'Harrying of the North', the memory of which lingered long after the events, so much so that William would still be referred to as 'Billy the Bastard' in a number of Yorkshire villages as late as the 1930s. The whole of the region was laid to waste from coast to coast, with the hunted taking refuge in the wooded valleys of Yorkshire, where they perished through starvation and exposure. Many of those who did not die sold themselves into slavery, driven by terrible hunger. For many years afterwards the rotting corpses of the dead caused by the famine littered the land and the county was desolate.

When William arrived at York he was to find no resistance. In fact, he was welcomed with open arms and given the key to the city. During the Christmas of 1069 he wintered at the city, before continuing with his manhunt. William made York his base and strengthened its defences; he also constructed two motte and bailey castles, each on opposite sides of the River Ouse. Of these castles only the remains of Clifford's Tower are still standing, while the castle to the south, which once stood on Baile Hill, has long since disappeared.

Although William was described by a chronicler as a 'very stern and violent man, so that no one dared do anything contrary to his will', the same writer went on to say that the Conqueror had made the country secure so that an honest man could go about his business confident that he could do so without fear of attack and no one would dare strike another, regardless of how aggrieved he felt. But perhaps his most enduring legacy was the compilation of the *Domesday Book* in 1086, as the history of many an English village would start with an entry in the book.

ST MARY'S ABBEY

The Abbey of St Mary was first founded in 1055, and was originally dedicated to St Olave (St Olaf Haraldson, who had been a king of Norway in the early 11th century). In 1088 the

A plaque in the abbey wall commemorating the opening of a gate in the wall, which was done in honour of Princess Margaret, the future mother of Mary, Queen of Scots, when she stayed in York as she journeyed north to marry James IV of Scotland.

abbey was relocated by William II and at the same time was rededicated to St Mary. In time, it would become the largest and richest Benedictine monastery in the north of England.

It is said that the abbots of St Mary's were very worldly and the abbey would often feature

The 14th-century timber-framed Hospitium, which was once used as the guesthouse for St Mary's.

The ruins of St Mary's Abbey Church.

St Leonard's Hospital was founded by King Athelstan to commemorate his victory at Brunanburh in 937. It was once the largest hospital in England. Originally, it had been dedicated to St Peter, but when it was rebuilt in the 12th century by King Stephen he changed its name to St Leonard's.

in early mediaeval ballads of Robin Hood, with the abbot named as the outlaw's nemesis. With the Dissolution of the Monasteries in 1539, the abbey was closed and subsequently destroyed. Today, all that remains are some fragments of the ruinous Abbey Church, the West Gate, the Pilgrims' Hospitium and the stunning 14th-century King's Manor (with its outstanding Jacobean doorway).

ALL SAINTS CHURCH – NORTH STREET

Evidence suggests that there was a church at the site of the present All Saints Church a long time prior to the Norman invasion and in all probability it would have been a simple rectangular construction. However, the first reference to this church is in 1089, when Ralph Paganell, who was the layman to the Benedictine Priory of the Holy Trinity, granted patronage to the rectory. With a growing population at the end of the 12th century, an aisle was added to the church and fragments of Roman columns found at the site were used in its construction. The chancel was reconstructed in the 13th century in the Early English style and a second aisle was added at the same time. In the early 14th century the area became popular with the city's elite and consequently a number of large, fine houses were constructed near the church. The church was to benefit from this increased prosperity as money was lavished upon it and subsequently the east end was rebuilt.

At the end of the 14th century major work began on the church, which culminated in the

St Leonard's once covered a vast area. However, all that remains today is the ruinous chapel.

A turret on the city walls.

building that we see today. The tower, octagon and 120-foot spire were added and no expense was spared. It is thought that the whole of the church, except the easternmost part, might have been demolished at this time. Money was left in the will of Richard Byrd in 1394 for the fabric of the church. By 1410 the tower and spire were complete, but with most of the funds exhausted work on the rest of the building slowed down. The roof was still not complete by 1440 and it was only through bequests of tiles and lead that the work was finally completed. Eventually, in 1470, the church was finished when the lavish ceilings over the chancel and aisle were installed. At this time, the church might have had as many as five separate altars (although we only know definitely of four): the altar to the Blessed Virgin Mary, the altar to St Nicholas, the altar to St Thomas the Martyr and the altar to St James the Great. These, however, would be removed during the Reformation and the interior of the building would be altered beyond all recognition. Originally, the church would have employed a large number of priests to serve the altars, but with their loss the need to maintain a large number of staff was removed and, by the end of the 16th century, the church was served by a single rector and a lay parish clerk.

Today worship still takes place at this church, which has been hallowed for over a millennium.

THE CITY WALLS

One of York's most outstanding features is its City Walls, which are probably the best in the United Kingdom. We were, however, very nearly robbed of the opportunity to study their splendour when, at the beginning of the 19th century, plans were being made by the city fathers to demolish them. Had it not been for the dedication and sheer determination of the artist William Etty RA (1787–1849), they would certainly have been destroyed. His tireless campaigning saved the walls for future

generations to enjoy and marvel at. He also helped fund their restoration from his own pocket.

York's first walls were erected in AD71 by the Romans, who constructed them as a defence around their fort. The walls covered an area of approximately 50 acres. In the early third century the Roman Emperor Septimus Severus ordered

Standing outside the City Art Gallery in Exhibition Square is the weather-worn statue of William Etty RA (1787–1849) by George Walker Miburn, which was sculpted in 1910. Etty's love of the city of his birth prompted him to save the city walls.

The Multangular Tower is York's only remaining Roman tower. For many years it had been called Elrondyng, until in the 18th century it was realised that it was of Roman origin.

that eight defensive towers shpuld be added to the walls. These towers were substantial 10-sided structures, which were nearly 30 feet tall.

When the Danes occupied the city in 867 they were to demolish the majority of the walls and all but one of the towers, which by then were in a poor state of repair. The only tower to remain was the Multangular Tower, which stands to this day in the Museum Gardens. The top part of the tower, with its arrow-slits, was added in the Middle Ages.

The foundations of the Roman walls were used to form part of the later walls, which were constructed from the 12th to the 14th century. The walls are punctuated by four major gatehouses or 'bars': Monk Bar, Bootham Bar, Walmgate Bar and Micklegate Bar. There are also two smaller bars, which are Fishergate Bar

City Walls.

Opposite: A view along the city walls with the Minster standing majestically in the far distance.

An ice house below the city walls: each winter, ice was collected and stored here for the coming months.

and Victoria Bar. Following riots in 1489, Fishergate Bar was blocked up, but in 1827 it was reopened and it still provides access for pedestrians. Victoria Bar was a 19th-century addition and was opened in 1838.

It is still possible to walk along the top of the walls and enjoy the magnificent views of this historic city. For this we can be forever thankful for the love and foresight of one man, whose rather weather-worn statue now stands outside the City Art Gallery on Exhibition Square: William Etty RA.

YORK MINSTER

It is no exaggeration to say that the magnificent York Minster is one of Britain's iconic buildings and each year it attracts hundreds of thousands of visitors from around the world. Work first began on the present edifice in 1230 and took a little over 200 years to complete. This was not the first church to have stood on this spot, for there has been a place of worship here since 627, when a wooden structure was hastily constructed so that Edwin, the king of Northumbria, could be baptised by St Paulinus. Ten years later a more substantial stone structure was erected by King Oswald and this was dedicated to St Peter. But, sadly, the church soon fell into disrepair and by the year 670 the dilapidated building was in a sorry state. In that year, York was visited by the English bishop St Wilfrid who, appalled at the condition of this

Monk Bar: dating from the 13th century, it is the tallest of the four bars. It was once assumed that it was named after the 17th-century General Monk, but it is now thought that it is a reference to the monks from the neighbouring abbey. It has the city's only working portcullis, which was last lowered in 1953 for the coronation of Elizabeth II.

holy building, soon galvanised a programme of repair and renovation. At the same time the famous St Peter's School and library were established, which by the eighth century were famous throughout Christendom.

In 741 disaster struck when the church was destroyed by fire (this was to be the first of a number of times when York Minster was destroyed, or nearly destroyed, by fire). The church was rebuilt on a grander scale, which was to include no fewer than 30 altars. By the ninth century the church had fallen somewhat into obscurity after the Danish invasions and it was not until the next century that its fortunes began to change, once more for the better. Although many ancient Christian centres would have suffered greatly during these dangerous times, there is no evidence that the Danes who eventually settled in the region were totally against Christianity. In fact, Guthfrith, the first known king of Danish Northumbria, was a Christian and when he died on 24 August 895 at York he was buried in the Minster.

During William the Conqueror's 'Harrying of the North' in 1069 the Minster suffered damage, and although repairs were undertaken the following year with the arrival of the first Norman archbishop, the building was destroyed five years later by the Danes. Work began to rebuild it in 1080 by Thomas of Bayeux, the Archbishop of York. The new building was 365 feet long and built in the Norman style (today the foundations of this Norman church can be seen in the Foundations Exhibition). Fire was to damage this building once more in 1137, which resulted in the choir and crypt being rebuilt in 1154; at the same time a large chapel dedicated to St Sepulchre was added to the nave.

By the mid-12th century it had become fashionable to build cathedrals in the Gothic style and when Walter de Gray became the Archbishop of York in 1215 he was determined to build a Gothic Minster which would rival Canterbury. During the construction the

Opposite:
The breathtaking York Minster at night.

Standing at the front of the Minster is a model which represents the city.

central tower collapsed in 1407, and this was eventually rebuilt after strengthening the piers. The work on this Gothic masterpiece, which would eventually remove all traces of the Norman structure, was finished in the 15th century.

The English Reformation of the 16th century brought with it the Minster's first Anglican archbishop. At the same time the church lost much of its lands and many of the cathedral's treasures were taken. During the reign of Elizabeth I further loss and damage was suffered by the Minster when tombs, windows and altars were destroyed in an attempt to remove all traces of the Roman Catholic Church. In 1644 the City of York fell to the Parliamentarian forces, but fortunately this beautiful building was spared further damage by the intervention of Sir Thomas Fairfax, commander-in-chief of Cromwell's New Model Army. The 18th century brought further restoration to the cathedral and in 1730 work started on totally replacing the floor with patterned marble; the work took six years to complete. In 1802 a major programme of restoration was undertaken.

The awesome towers of the Minster loom above the rooftops.

On 1 February 1829 tragedy struck when the arsonist Jonathan Martin set the Minster on fire. This destroyed the majority of the interior woodwork: the organ, the pulpit, the stalls, the galleries and the bishop's throne were all lost in the flames. In addition, a large part of the roof was also destroyed. Martin was arrested five days later and tried at York Castle. He was defended by Henry Brougham, who had gained fame when he had defended Queen Caroline in 1821 against claims that she had committed adultery. The jury found him guilty and he would have faced the hangman's noose if it had not been for the judge, who overruled the verdict by declaring Martin insane (Martin had maintained that a buzzing sound coming from the organ had disturbed him). He was detained in Bethlem Royal Hospital (otherwise known as Bedlam) until his death nine years later.

An accidental fire 11 years later did more damage to the building, and left the nave, south-west tower and the south aisle roofless. The cathedral's troubles were far from over, as mounting debts culminated in the suspension of services in 1850. However, help came eight years later when the Very Reverend Augustus Duncombe, Dean of York, began to revive this grand building. The 20th century saw more restoration work and in 1967 a survey revealed that the structure was in grave danger of collapsing. The work to strengthen the building would cost £2 million, while a further £2.5 million was required to repair the damage from a fire in 1984. Today, restoration continues on this delightful Gothic edifice, which will cost an estimated £23 million.

As we have seen, this remarkable building has withstood numerous attempts to destroy it, either by design or by accident, and it still stands as one of the finest examples of Gothic architecture in the land. This much loved cathedral is truly an iconic edifice. The largest of its type in Northern Europe, it possesses the largest expanse of mediaeval stained glass in the world. The magnificent Minster has been drawing visitors since the Middle Ages, either as pilgrims or simply as tourists, wishing to admire the awesome and breathtaking beauty of this outstanding structure: a York without its Minster would be unthinkable.

Far left: Part of the former Archbishop's Palace, which is now used as the Minster library. On 8 September 1483 Richard III's son was invested as Prince of Wales in this building.

Left: A restored capital at the top of one of the columns.

BISHOPTHORPE AND THE ARCHBISHOP'S PALACE

In 1226 Archbishop Walter de Grey bought the village of Thorpe St Andrew, where, after demolishing an old manor house, he created his new palace. He changed the village name to Bishopthorpe. Prior to this the Archbishop's Palace had been located in the grounds of the Minster, and the remains of this can still be seen today. It is thought that the old palace dates back to 1154, and today it is used as the Minster library.

The palace at Bishopthorpe has remained the residence of the Archbishop of York from 1241 to the present day, with the exception of 10 years during the protectorate in the mid-16th century, and again during the interregnum, when Britain was a republic, from 1649 to 1660.

Over the centuries, the palace has undergone

Far left: In the Dean's Park, next to the Minster, stand the remains of a colonnade from the former Archbishop's Palace.

Left: The beautiful Gothic gatehouse to the Archbishop's Palace at Bishopthorpe, which was designed by the famous architect John Carr in the 1760s.

The entrance to the Treasurer's House.

a number of alterations and additions. In the late 15th century a north wing was added by Archbishop Rotherham, and in the 1760s the renowned architect John Carr was commissioned by Archbishop Drummond. Carr created a Gothic stable block and a stunning gatehouse.

Today, the palace is more than the residence for the archbishop, for it is also used for a number of functions, such as working offices, meeting rooms, charity open days and retreats, to name but a few.

THE TREASURER'S HOUSE

The Treasurer's House was built on the site where the official residence of the Treasurers of York Minster once stood. The original building was constructed in 1419; however, the present building is the result of many centuries of additions and alterations. In 1547 the office of the Treasurer was abolished as a direct result of the Reformation and the property became the property of the Crown. In 1565 it was sold to Thomas Young, who was the archbishop at that

time. He was also President of the Council of the North, which was a Yorkshire-based seat of the government that had first been created in 1484 by Richard III: this meant that Thomas was an extremely powerful man.

Detail of the Treasurer's House.

The Golden Bible is a sign above a shop on Stonegate: in the 18th and 19th centuries this was York's leading bookshop. It also had its own printing press and it was from here that in 1759 John Hinxman published the first two volumes of Laurence Sterne's Tristram Shandy.

In the early 17th century the Young family rebuilt the main part of the house. The family were to own the property for a number of generations, until in 1648 they sold it to Sir Thomas Fairfax (1612–1671). It was later sold to Dr Jaques Sterne, the uncle of the writer Laurence Sterne of Shandy Hall, Coxwold, and Archdeacon of Cleveland and Percentor of York Minster. He was a powerful clergyman, but notoriously mean-tempered. He had strong political views and was a committed Whig; he persuaded his nephew to take up political writing, which would eventually lead to a major falling out between the two men. Dr Sterne would make life difficult for his nephew and would take any opportunity to stand in his way of progress.

In the 18th century the Dutch astronomer John Goodricke carried out his observations from the Treasurer's House while living in York, between 1782 and 1786. He is regarded as one of the greatest astronomers of his age. Although deaf and dumb from childhood after contracting scarlet fever, he would not allow these disabilities to hinder him. He is best known for his observations of the variable star Algol (Beta Persei) which he made in 1782 and his hypothesis on the mechanism of variable stars. In May 1783 he presented his findings to the Royal Society, and in the same year he was awarded the Copley Medal for his work. On 16 May 1786 he was elected a Fellow of the Royal Society, but sadly he was never to learn of this as he died four days later from pneumonia. He is buried in Hunsingore, North Yorkshire.

In 1897 the house was bought by Frank Green. He had made his fortune by selling a heating boiler, which was to his own design, called the Green's Economiser. He was a true

Attached to the wall of the Treasurer's House is a plaque which commemorates the Dutch astronomer John Goodricke, who made a number of his observations from a window in this building.

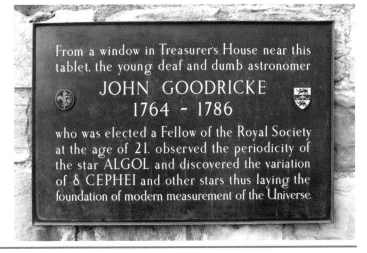

From a window in Treasurer's House near this tablet, the young deaf and dumb astronomer
JOHN GOODRICKE
1764 – 1786
who was elected a Fellow of the Royal Society at the age of 21, observed the periodicity of the star ALGOL and discovered the variation of δ CEPHEI and other stars thus laying the foundation of modern measurement of the Universe.

eccentric who used his wealth to purchase a number of properties in the Minster yard, including St William's College. He would restore these buildings to his own high standards, although not everyone would agree with his interpretation, especially when he removed the ceiling in the Great Hall of the Treasurer's House to create a gallery. It was Frank who was responsible for much of the present interior. In 1930, after retiring from the family business, he moved to Somerset. He left the house and its entire contents to the National Trust. It appears, however, that he was furious when he learnt that they had moved some of the furniture from where he had placed it, and threatened that should they ever move 'even so much as a chair leg' that he would haunt the culprit till his dying day.

In 1953, while working in the cellar, a young plumber called Harry Martindale was disturbed by the sound of a horn being blown and was alarmed to see the ghostly form of Roman soldiers marching past him. The group of soldiers appeared dirty and bedraggled, and what made the sight even more astounding was that they were cut off at the knees. It was later discovered that a couple of feet below the existing floor were the remains of a Roman road, which would account for the missing lower parts of their legs. Initially Martindale was ridiculed when he told what he had witnessed and a number of historians were also sceptical. His description of the armour that the soldiers were wearing did not match with what the academics said it should be. Later research, however, revealed that his details of the armament and even the colour of the kilts which the soldiers wore was completely accurate, and even his doubters were forced to admit that perhaps he had been telling the truth.

WILLIAM OF YORK (1110–1154)

Great-nephew of King Stephen, and said to be great-grandson of William the Conqueror, it is highly probable that William FitzHerbert's royal

connections were instrumental in his obtaining the position of Archbishop of York. They could not have been a hindrance, for after a meteoric rise through the ecclesiastical ranks he was elected archbishop in January 1141. Unfortunately, his appointment had not received approval from the Vatican, and Pope Eugene III, who was a Cistercian, had favoured Henry Murdac, who also belonged to the Order. William was, therefore, deposed in 1147 and the favoured Murdac elected in his place. King Stephen was understandably furious and, refusing to accept his great-nephew's deposition, prevented Murdac from taking up residence in York.

It was not long, however, before the position became vacant once more when, in 1153, Murdac

Opposite: St John the Baptist's Church, Hunsingore: the final resting place of John Goodricke.

Located above the main entrance of St William's College is a statue of the saint.

died, shortly followed by Pope Eugene III. There was now a new pontiff at the head of the Roman Church, Anastasius IV. William FitzHerbert wasted no time in heading off to Rome to plead with the new Pope. His appeal must have been successful, for on 20 December 1153 he was reappointed Archbishop of York.

On his return to York he was greeted by rapturous crowds, which had gathered to witness the triumphal procession. There were so many standing on the Ouse Bridge that it collapsed under the strain, hurling the spectators into the river below. Fortunately, no one was drowned, and this was seen by many as a miracle, which they attributed to William. A month after his celebrated arrival, however, the archbishop lay dead from suspected poisoning. The finger of blame was pointed at an archdeacon of York named Osbert, who was summoned to the royal court, where he was to stand trial before the king. However, before the trial could take place King Stephen died and it never went ahead.

Within a few months of William's death a number of miracles had happened and in 1223 sweet-smelling oil flowed from his tomb. On 18 March 1226 he was canonised by Pope Honorius III, and in 1283 his relics were placed in a shrine behind the high altar in the Minster, where they remained until the Reformation. His remains were discovered in the 1960s and have been placed in the crypt in the Minster. The Feast of St William is celebrated in York on 8 June; this day being the date of his death.

CLIFFORD'S TOWER

Although William the Conqueror had beaten Harold at Hastings in 1066 and the prize of the Crown of England was now unquestionably his, he was not destined to have everything his own way, and the north proved to be troublesome. It is not known how much William would have known about York before his invasion of England – he would at least have known that the city had an archbishop, and he may have even known that it was a city in the north of England. Much more than that we can only surmise, but two years after his invasion the city of York would play a significant role in his subjugation of the north.

When he eventually arrived in York in 1068 he found, according to the chronicler Orderic Vitalis, a city which was seething with discontent. For the

The infamous Clifford's Tower was the scene of many executions.

previous two centuries it had been a Viking city, and for all intents and purposes it had been a city which had been free from royal interference and able to administer its own affairs. This was about to change with the arrival of William.

Determined to bring York firmly under his control, he immediately set about building a castle. A second one followed a year later. Although it has always been believed that he built Clifford's Tower first, we cannot be totally certain of this. We do, however, know that it was originally constructed to the standard Norman design of a high central mound called a motte, on which was placed a wooden keep and below which stood a defensive wooden enclosure called a bailey.

In 1069 the castles were burnt to the ground and the garrison massacred during a local uprising, which was supported by King Swein of Denmark, who had arrived with a large fleet of ships. William was quick to act and immediately marched north to crush this uprising. He began a military campaign which became known as the 'Harrying of the North'. The scale of his reprisals is unclear; however, contemporary chroniclers recorded that the devastation was harsh even by the standards of the day. Orderic Vitalis wrote that on his deathbed William confessed to treating the 'fair' people with unreasonable severity and that he murdered thousands of innocent people, both young and old, burnt houses and crops, and slaughtered their sheep and cattle.

Even accounting for exaggeration as the tales were told and retold, this was a 'scorched-earth' policy of devastating proportions and one which would live in the memories of the people for many generations to come.

After the uprising had finally been suppressed, the Normans rebuilt the castles. In 1190 the wooden keep was once again burnt to the ground during a siege when the Jewish community, who had taken refuge within its walls, set fire to it in preference to being captured alive by the mob. On

the orders of Henry III, the castle was rebuilt in stone in 1244 when the Scots threatened to invade England. It is not known how the castle became known as Clifford's Tower; some believe that it was named after Roger de Clifford, who was hanged there in 1322.

As well as its military function, it was also the base for the Sheriff of Yorkshire and the centre of law and order in the region. Often criminals and traitors were hanged from the castle's battlements as a visible deterrent to others. The political leader of the 'Pilgrimage of Grace', Robert Aske, was hanged there in 1536 on orders from Henry VIII. In the 16th century Robert Redhead, the tower keeper, was hanged there after it was discovered that he had been selling off the castle's stonework. Some 10 layers had gone before anyone had noticed that the battlements and turrets were slowly disappearing.

In 1642 the English Civil War broke out and the Royalists under Henry Clifford, Earl of Cumberland, immediately took control of the city of York. He repaired the castle and strengthened the walls so that they would support the weight of the heavy cannon. Two years later the city was under siege. Just over a month after the siege had begun, Prince Rupert arrived and was able to force the besiegers to withdraw. Unfortunately, the next day he was defeated in the largest and bloodiest battle of the war – Marston Moor.

The city found itself once more under siege and on 14 July 1644 it surrendered to the Parliamentarian forces. The Royalists were allowed to march out of the city with full honour, after which the Roundheads proceeded to destroy Clifford's Tower. After the Restoration of Charles II the castle was repaired, and at around that time some heraldic panels were added, containing the king's coat of arms and those of the Clifford family. These panels can be found above the main entrance. The last person to garrison the castle was Henry Clifford and it is thought more probable that it was through him the castle was named and not in memory of the execution of Roger de Clifford.

At around 10pm on 23 April 1684 (St George's Day) the castle's magazine exploded, destroying the interior and reducing the tower to its exterior walls. There is much evidence to suggest that this was not an accident. It had long been the wish of the citizens of York to be rid of the castle, or the 'Minced Pie' as it was referred to. Not only was no one killed in the explosion, but also, with extraordinary good fortune, the entire garrison had removed their belongings prior to the disaster. Afterwards the ruined tower became no more than an ornamental feature in the grounds of a large house, which had by that time been built nearby.

In the 18th century three new buildings were built: the County Gaol, the Assize Courts and a Female Prison. In 1825, after both Clifford's Tower and the large house had been purchased, a number of new prison buildings were erected and the whole area was used as a prison for the next 100 years. All these new buildings would eventually be demolished in 1935.

Today Clifford's Tower is owned by English Heritage, but recently there have been moves to build a retail development on the land around the tower. However, there has been much opposition to the plans from various quarters, including local people, visitors, business people, academics and some Jewish groups. So far their protestations have enjoyed some success and the tower has escaped becoming part of a retail park.

THE MASSACRE OF YORK (SHABBAT HA-GADOL)

By the mid-to-late 12th century York had a small but thriving Jewish community, who made their living as moneylenders. They had initially been attracted to the city as it possessed an important royal castle, which would have given them a feeling of security and a refuge in times of trouble, for as moneylenders they attracted much resentment. Business would have been extremely lucrative for them as there were many lords, gentry and religious houses in the area, all of whom would have made extensive use of their financial services. Even Henry II had borrowed from them, which

At the foot of the hill on which Clifford's Tower stands there is a plaque which remembers those who died at the Massacre of Shabbat ha-Gadol in 1190.

would no doubt have given them a certain veneer of respectability.

There was, however, a growing resentment against the Jews, not only in York, but throughout the country as a whole. This had been brought about in part by the Crusades, for by this time Christian Europe was embroiled in the Fourth Crusade and was attempting to recapture Palestine and free the Sepulchre of Jesus from the grip of the Moslems. It was inevitable that this would lead to hatred of non-Christians, and it was not long before the Jewish communities became the target of this animosity. The masses denounced them, calling them 'the killers of Christ living in our midst'.

However, it was the death of Henry II in July 1189 that brought things rapidly to a head. His eldest son, Richard, was crowned king of England and during his coronation at Westminster a deputation of Jews arrived bearing gifts for the new monarch. However, they were refused entry and, to further add to their humiliation, they were pelted with stones by a mob, which had gathered to witness the ceremony. A rumour spread like wildfire throughout the angry mob that the new king had ordered the destruction of the Jews. It was completely false, but by this point feelings were running so high that 24 hours of violent rioting ensued. Immediately, the houses of the Jews became targets and their straw roofs were set alight. Those who managed to escape the flames were either butchered or offered salvation if they were willing to be baptised; some took their own lives rather than betray their faith.

Richard I was furious and sent in troops to quell the rioting. Eventually, law and order were restored. To send out a clear message that he would not tolerate the attacking of Jews, the king had three of the rioters hanged. For a short time a fragile peace was restored, but as soon as Richard crossed the Channel to join the Crusades fresh riots broke out. Throughout the country, the Jewish communities found themselves once more in peril.

In March 1190, a group of men broke into the house of the late Benedict of York, who had died while in Northampton from wounds received in the initial riots. They slaughtered his petrified widow and children, and after plundering the house they set fire to it. York's Jewish community was terrified and with their leader, a man called Joseph, they sought refuge in the royal castle. Any feeling of security would have been short-lived when it was discovered that the warden had left the stronghold. There was a fear that he might have gone to betray them to the besieging mob. When he returned, the warden discovered that the entrance to the building had been barred; this resulted in him calling in the assistance of the Sheriff of the county, Richard Malebys. The Sheriff was deeply in debt to the Jews and, seeing this as an ideal opportunity to rid himself his liabilities, he took command of the siege.

The passion of the crowds was roused further by a monk in white robes, who preached before them and incited them with words of encouragement. Their fury was further inflamed when falling masonry hit the priest, killing him outright. By now rations were growing short and the Jews faced a grim dilemma: face death either by starvation, or at the hands of the mob which awaited them outside. A third option was to convert to Christianity and be baptised, but to many this was unthinkable and, indeed, their religious leader beseeched them to take their own lives rather than betray their faith. It was the feast of Shabbat ha-Gadol when the massacre was to take place. The castle had been set alight and by dawn it had been recaptured. All those who were still alive were murdered.

The mob then made its way to the cathedral, where the records of debts were stored for safe keeping. Demanding that they were handed over, they were burnt there and then in the sanctuary. With the destruction of the records the fury of the mob abated; it was as though their anger was spent with this final act. The mob simply went home and peace was restored in the city. The massacre in York had cost the lives of 150 Jews and today a plaque stands next to Clifford's Tower, reminding us of that dark event in the history of York.

On King Richard's return to England, he introduced a new system of registering all debts by recording them in duplicate. It was not in the interest of the Crown for debts to be cleared in this violent manner, as the king received much revenue through taxation of debts and was, in effect, a silent partner of the moneylenders.

THE MERCHANT ADVENTURERS' HALL

On the banks of the River Foss stands the Merchant Adventurers' Hall. This magnificent mediaeval building is regarded by many to be one of the finest examples of an English guildhall still in existence. It was originally constructed as a hospital in 1357 by a number of the city's important citizens, who had joined together to form a religious fraternity, and at the same time they formed a trading association: the Mercers' Guild. They dedicated the hall to the Blessed Virgin, and as well as a place to pray, they used the building for their business transactions, social meetings and to look after the poor.

Using many local materials, it took four years to complete. As many as 100 oak trees were felled in the Vale of York for the timbers of the hall. Although it was to increase the final cost, the roof was tiled rather than thatched, as this was considered much safer and reduced the risk of fire, and the merchants felt that it was money well spent.

By 1430 the Mercers' Guild had become known as the Fellowship of Mercers. In 1581 Elizabeth I granted their incorporation by royal charter and they became the Company of Merchant Adventurers. Many of the guild's members went on to hold the prestigious office of Mayor of York. This was an extremely powerful position, for the mayor would have almost autocratic powers over the inhabitants of the city.

The stunning timber-framed Merchant Adventurers' Hall stands in Fossgate.

Detail of the Merchant Adventurers' Hall as seen through the cherry blossom.

For almost 600 years the guild had almost total control over the city's trade, making it an exceedingly powerful trading association. In 1835, however, their restrictive hold over the city's commerce was finally abolished by an Act of Parliament. During the height of its powers it was impossible for a non-member to run a shop. It was no easy matter gaining entry into this elite body, as Mary Tuke was to discover in the 18th century. For a number of years she fought a battle with the Company of Merchant Adventurers when she opened a grocery shop in the Walmgate area of the city. They did not consider her eligible for membership, as she was neither a widow nor a daughter of a member. They imposed fines on her on numerous

Appearing above Lendal Bridge can be seen Lendal Tower.

occasions in a bid to stop her trading, but she carried on regardless, until in 1732 her persistence paid off and they allowed her to trade. A year later she moved her shop near to the Friends' Meeting House in Castlegate. After her death her son William Tuke took over the business, which by this time was highly successful in dealing in tea. In 1860 Tuke and Co. was joined by Henry Isaac Rowntree, who two years later bought the cocoa and chocolate department from the company and Rowntree's was born.

The Company of Merchant Adventurers is no longer a trading association, but today holds the hall in trust. Although it is now a museum, it still plays an active role in both the business and civic life of the city.

LENDAL TOWER AND BARKER TOWER

Built in the 14th century on the opposing sides of the River Ouse, the towers of Lendal and Barker were originally constructed to prevent merchant ships from slipping into the city without first paying a toll. A huge chain was hung between the two towers, acting as a barrier. Standing further along the river were another pair of towers, Davy Tower and the now demolished Hyngbrig Tower, which also had a chain hung between them.

By the mid-16th century the chains were considered unnecessary and in 1553 they were sold off. In the 17th century Lendal Tower became the city's first waterworks. Water was pumped directly from the river through pipes, which had been made from tree trunks. For the next 150 years this system was considered adequate for the city's needs, but with increasing demands a new waterworks became essential. In 1846 a new site was found in Clifton.

The tower had been rented from the city to York Waterworks for 500 years at an annual rent of two peppercorns. As the lease does not run out until 2177, this rent is still paid each year at

the peppercorn ceremony. Today Lendal Tower is used as an office block.

Barker Tower has also had a number of uses: a mortuary, a shop and even an artist's studio. Today it is known as the North Street Postern.

Opposite Lendal Tower stands Barker Tower.

The timbers of the Merchant Taylors' Hall.

MERCHANT TAYLORS' HALL

By the late 14th century there were around 128 master tailors working in York. They had not at this time formed themselves into a guild, but a number of them began to worship in the Minster at an altar that was dedicated to their patron saint – St John the Baptist. From this loosely knit fraternity was born the Guild of Taylors. As they became wealthy they grew in confidence and eventually built their own guildhall.

York had entered a boom time for the woollen industry and the high quality woollen goods which were being produced in the city were in high demand. It was not long before they were dominating the market, with the obvious result that it was attracting great wealth to the city. The citizens found themselves at the peak of their power and fortunes, and at its height York was the second largest city in England. However, by the late 15th century this rising star was well and truly waning. York now faced dire economic problems, and although it was not the only city in England to be in the grips of a recession, its ability to ride out the storm had become so impaired that it would never again experience the dizzying heights which it had enjoyed in the previous two centuries. The city was being ruled harshly by Edward IV, who was unable to forgive the citizens of York for their Lancastrian sympathies. To add to their problems the population had fallen by almost half and the woollen industry was now nearly non-existent. Many of the weavers had left the city, tired of its strict regulations, and moved to the unincorporated townships such as Halifax, Leeds and Wakefield.

The brick exterior of the Merchant Taylors' Hall dates from the 17th century. In the early 1700s the glass painter Henry Gyles (1640–1709) created two stained-glass windows for the hall, both including the guild's crest of arms, and one of them bearing a portrait of Queen Anne. Today, the hall is used as a venue for various events, such as weddings and dinners.

BARLEY HALL

Dating from about 1360, the hall was originally built as a York townhouse for Nostell Priory. In 1430 a new wing was added and shortly afterwards the building became the home of William Snawsell, who as well as being a prosperous goldsmith, was also Lord Mayor of York in 1468. As a leading citizen he represented the city when the Lancastrian Henry VI took the throne in 1470; but a year later he was forced to buy a royal pardon when the Yorkist Edward IV became king. Snawsell was later to become a friend of Richard III and when the king was killed on the battlefield at Bosworth on 27 August 1485, it was his name which headed a list of councillors who recorded the news '... *through great treason of the Duke of Norfolk and many others that turned against him with many other lords and nobles of these north parts, was piteously slain and murdered, to the great heaviness of this city.*'

Barley Hall is of great significance to historians, for of the original 40 or so monastic houses which were once located in York, this is the only surviving. The hall was built by

Barley Hall: this magnificent building was once hidden beneath a modern façade.

Thomas de Dereford, who had been Prior of Nostell from 1337 to 1372. As Prior, he was expected to attend ceremonies and business meetings in the city, so it was considered essential for him to have a residence in York.

It is thought that by the 17th century the hall would no longer have been a single residence, but would have been split up into a number of smaller properties, which sometime over the next 200 years were converted into tradesmen's workshops. In the 1980s the building, which by this time had been covered with a modern façade, was derelict and due for demolition. Fortunately, the magnificent mediaeval building which lay hidden beneath its 20th-century shell was discovered and the building was saved.

YORK MYSTERY PLAYS (A MOVEABLE FEAST)

It is not recorded when the first performance of the York Mystery Plays was given, but it is thought that they may date back to the 12th century. Originally they were known as the Corpus Christi Plays, for they were performed on the Feast of Corpus Christi, which was a moveable feast held the Thursday after Trinity Sunday, between 23 May and 24 June.

They consist of a cycle of 48 English mystery plays, or pageants, which were performed by the guilds. Each play told a story from the Bible and covered every aspect from creation to the Last Judgement, and traditionally each of the separate guilds would be responsible for performing their own particular play.

Although the Feast of Corpus Christi was abolished in 1548 with the Reformation, by removing certain scenes which contained the Virgin Mary the plays continued for the next 21 years, until they were finally suppressed in 1569. It was not until after they had been prohibited that they received the name 'Mystery Plays' – the name refers to the guilds who performed them and is derived from the Latin word *Ministerium*, meaning a trade or craft.

The plays were traditionally performed on wagons that were wheeled through the streets of York and would stop at various points along the way for the plays to be acted out. In 1951 they were revived and performed at St Mary's Abbey in a modified form. Since then they have been performed on a four-yearly cycle, and in 2000 they were held in the Minster.

ST WILLIAM'S COLLEGE

Work on the construction of St William's College began in 1465 on the instructions of Edward IV. It was to be the home of the Minster's Chantry Priests, whose principal job was to receive advanced payments so that prayers might be said for their departed benefactors, or as an insurance premium to ensure a place in heaven. When this dubious practice came to an end with the Reformation the building became redundant.

In March 1642 Charles I and his court arrived in York as refugees fleeing from London,

The impressive timber-framed St William's College, which was built in 1461.

The main entrance to St William's College.

A close examination of the main door reveals the trademark mouse of Robert Thompson, the prolific 20th-century furniture maker.

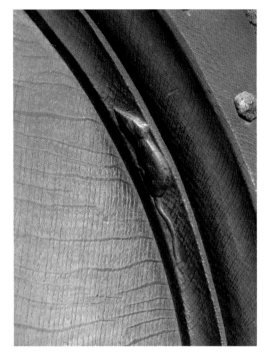

where their position had been made untenable by angry mobs, who had been incited by Parliament. His arrival had not been entirely welcomed by the citizens of York, but even so crowds thronged both sides of the streets to greet him. He stayed for six months in the city, during which time he set up his printing press in St William's College. It was from here that he would mount his Royalist propaganda campaign. His printers, Robert Barker and Stephen Bulkeley, would produce pamphlets, which were distributed throughout the country.

The building was restored at the beginning of the 20th century by Frank Green, and today the building can be hired as a venue for conferences and banquets.

KING'S MANOR

The King's Manor was originally the abbot's house and was built in the 13th century. The building was part of St Mary's Abbey but after the Dissolution of the Monasteries, it became the property of the Crown. Until 1642 the Council of the North was held there. Over the years the Manor was gradually extended, with much of the construction work being done

The breathtaking Jacobean doorway of King's Manor, with its Stuart royal crest.

during the reign of Elizabeth I. The Earl of Huntingdon, who was President of the Council from 1572 to 1595, was responsible for the addition of the residential wings and a service building. However, Henry VIII also made some additions to the building, when he added a wine cellar using stone taken from the abbey.

The property was especially popular with the Stuarts, who regularly stayed there while travelling between Edinburgh and London. The magnificent main entrance is Jacobean and shows the coat of arms of James I and Charles II. After 1641 and the abolition of the Council of the North, the building gradually fell into decline. During the Siege of York in 1644 the property received some minor damage, and in the late 17th century it became the residence of the military governors of the city. Shortly afterwards it was used as a private boarding school for girls.

In 1833 the Yorkshire School for the Blind was founded at the Manor, and it was gradually restored and enlarged. In the 1890s a gymnasium and a cloister were added and in

Along the Shambles stands the shrine to St Margaret Clitherow.

1900 the architect Walter Brierley constructed the Principal's House (today this is the Centre for Mediaeval Studies). In 1958 the Blind School moved to Tadcaster Road, and the property was acquired by York City Council. Five years later it was leased to the university. Today, it is the home of the Department of Archaeology, Mediaeval Studies and 18th-century Studies.

MARGARET CLITHEROW (1556–1586)

Born in 1556, Margaret Clitherow née Middleton had been brought up a Protestant and was baptised in St Martin-le-Grand. At the age of 15 she married John Clitherow, who was a prosperous local butcher on the Shambles. In 1572 she witnessed the execution of Thomas Percy, the 7th Earl of Northumberland, for his part in the rising of the Northern earls in 1569 under the Catholic banner. This event had a profound effect on the young Margaret and shortly afterwards she was converted to Catholicism by Dorothy, the wife of Dr Thomas Vavasour (1536–1585).

Her new faith would bring her into conflict with the authorities on numerous occasions, which would often result in her imprisonment. She used these periods of incarceration to her advantage and she learnt to read and recite her service in Latin. In 1585 she was to find herself once again in trouble with the authorities, but this time she refused to stand trial. It is not known whether she was aware of the consequences of this refusal, for she now faced the death sentence. Had she agreed to a trial, as she had done on many occasions before, she would have faced imprisonment. A number of officials tried in vain to persuade her to show at least a little conformity. They stressed the barbarity of the ordeal she would face and hoped to shock her into a realisation of the gravity of her stance, but she stood resolute.

On Good Friday of 1586 she was put to death. The two sergeants whose task it was to execute the young lady were unable to face their duty and hired four beggars to carry out the sentence. She was stripped and laid naked on a small sharp rock, which was no bigger than a man's fist. A door was placed on top of her and this was loaded with rocks. The beggars were told to pile up the rocks slowly, so that she still could change her mind. However, 15 minutes later she died when her back broke.

*The stupendous
Guildhall.*

In 1970 Pope Paul VI canonised Margaret along with a number of other English and Welsh martyrs. Today a house which stands on the Shambles, and was once thought to have been her home, is the Shrine of St Margaret Clitherow. In fact, this was not her home – the actual property stands further down the Shambles.

GUILDHALL

Built in the 15th century, the Guildhall was intended as a meeting place for the guilds of York. The guilds, however, rarely used the building and in 1459 the City Corporation began meeting there. In 1483 the newly crowned Richard III was entertained at a feast in the Guildhall. It was here that, between October 1568 and January 1569, the Court of Enquiry investigated the charges against Mary, Queen of Scots. A trial in all but name, the English were careful not to use the word 'trial', as the queen of one country had no legal right to try another for a crime which had not been committed on English soil.

It was at the Guildhall that in 1648 the Scots received £200,000 from Parliament for their part in the English Civil War: it took them 12 days to count the money. This was only the first instalment, for in total they had been promised £500,000 for their support.

The building which today stands on the banks of the River Ouse is mainly a reconstruction, as the original was badly damaged during the Baedeker Blitz in 1942: this was the most destructive air raid on the city. It is said that Hitler had ordered the destruction of a number of English cities in response to the British raid on Lübeck. The cities chosen were those which had appeared in the Baedeker tourist guidebook – hence the name of the raid. Karl Baedeker had been a German publisher in Koblenz, who in the 19th century had produced a number of guidebooks which covered most of Europe.

In 1525 work started on St Michael le Belfrey, and it took John Forman, who was the master mason to the Minster, 11 years to complete this delightful church.

THE CHURCH OF ST MICHAEL LE BELFREY

The church of St Michael le Belfrey stands next to York Minster. The present building was constructed in 1525 on the site of a previous church, which dates back to 1294. This delightful church is unique in that all its architecture dates from the same period. It is perhaps most famous for being the place where Guy Fawkes was christened on 16 April 1570. But it was also where the famous English explorer Christopher Levett (also a native of York) had married the Reverend Robert More's daughter, Mercy More, in 1608.

GUY FAWKES (1570–1606)

Remember, remember the fifth of November
The Gunpowder treason and plot
I can think of no reason
Why the Gunpowder treason
Should ever be forgot.

These are the opening lines to a traditional rhyme that tells of the Gunpowder Plot, and an event which we still celebrate to this day. Although each year we burn the effigy of Guy on top of a bonfire, it was intended that he should be hung, drawn and quartered (the traditional form of execution for high treason). Guy Fawkes escaped the disembowelling part of his ordeal, leaping from the gallows while being hanged and consequently snapping his neck.

Guy was born on 13 April 1570 at High Petergate in York. His father Edward Fawkes was an official of the ecclesiastical courts, and later was to become an advocate of the consistory court of the Archbishop of York. Guy's mother Edith Blake had descended from wealthy merchants and prominent citizens of the city. On 16 April 1570 Guy was baptised at St Michael le Belfrey. He was educated at St Peter's School, which is one of the oldest schools in the United Kingdom, having being founded by St Paulinus in the seventh century. It was while at this school that he may have been first exposed to Catholicism, when he was taught by John Pulleyn, a suspected Catholic.

In 1579 his father died and three years later his mother remarried. His stepfather was Denis Bainbridge of Scotton, a well-known Catholic and resister to the authority of the state religion. There can be no doubt that his stepfather's influence was to play a significant part in Guy's conversion, which happened when he was around 16. In the same year in which he made his conversion, Margaret Clitherow was cruelly executed, so he would have been under no illusions about how dangerous it could be to be a Roman Catholic in England.

After leaving school he became a footman for Anthony Browne, 1st Viscount Montagu, who was a leading statesman. The post was

This public house was once the home of the Fawkes family and is where Guy Fawkes was born in 1570.

destined to be short-lived, as Browne took a dislike to the young Fawkes and soon dismissed him. However, he was soon re-employed by Browne's grandson, the 2nd Viscount Montagu, as a table waiter. In 1593 he set off to Flanders, where he enlisted in the Spanish Army, under the command of Archduke Albert of Austria. He spent the next 10 years fighting for the Spanish and the Catholic cause. It was during this time that he became an expert with explosives, and it was this expertise which would later make him an ideal candidate for the laying and detonating of the gunpowder.

The Gunpowder Plot had been the brainchild of Robert Catesby, and the plan was to kill James I, his family and most of the country's aristocracy during the state opening of Parliament at the Palace of Westminster. In May 1604 Guy Fawkes met with the other conspirators in a London inn called the Duck and Drake. It had long been the hope that Spain would come to the aid of the long-suffering Catholics in Britain. But Spain was already fighting too many wars and was deeply in debt and it was clear that help would not come from this quarter. In 1604, at the Hampton Court Conference, James I attacked both the Catholics and extreme Puritans.

It is thought that the initial plan was to dig a tunnel under the House of Lords, but the group soon realised that it would create an insurmountable problem of how to dispose of the great quantities of dirt and debris without arousing suspicion. Therefore, shortly after the tunnel was begun, it was abandoned. In all probability the tunnel was never started, for no evidence of one has ever been found. In March 1605 the men rented a cellar beneath the House of Lords and the task began of filling it with barrels of gunpowder. A total of 36 barrels were placed in the cellar, containing 1,800 pounds of gunpowder, ready for the state opening.

A number of the conspirators were concerned that fellow Catholics would die in the explosion and so on 26 October 1605 a letter was received by Lord Monteagle warning of the plot. Its contents were vague, but the authors hoped that it would be enough to prevent Catholic deaths. This proved to be the undoing of the plotters, for as soon as Monteagle received the letter he took it to Whitehall, where he showed it to Robert Cecil and a number of other ministers. Now warned of the plot, an immediate search was made of the cellars and the gunpowder was discovered. However, so as not to alert the conspirators, they left everything untouched.

Guy Fawkes had vowed, if necessary, to blow himself up and, as he was attempting to ignite the charge, he was suddenly surprised as the torch was seized from his hand. He was immediately arrested. For the next few days he was tortured in the Tower of London. On the orders of the king the torture was to be light at first, but if necessary they were to increase the severity.

On 31 January 1606 Guy Fawkes and a number of his fellow conspirators were executed. In 2002 he was ranked 30th in the list of the 100 Greatest Britons, although traditionally he has been a figure of hate and ridicule.

WILLIAM TUKE AND THE RETREAT

William Tuke was born on 24 March 1732 and went into the family business as a tea and coffee merchant, which had been started by his mother, Mary Tuke, in 1725. The Tukes were a leading Quaker family and William would play an active part in the Society of Friends. In 1790 a Quaker from Leeds called Hannah Mills had died in the York Asylum. She was a young widow, who had been suffering from 'melancholy' (today it would be known as clinical depression). The Quakers were appalled by the conditions that Hannah and her fellow patients had to endure; conditions which no human being should be subjected to, with patients being treated worse than animals. The Quakers believed that the humanity and inner light of a human being could never be extinguished, and were horrified at the barbarity of the common medical practices of the day, which included keeping the patients permanently shackled in manacles. They felt compelled to do something about this and enlisted the help of William.

It took two years of planning and collecting funds before he was finally ready, but in 1796 William opened the York Retreat. This was to revolutionise the treatment of the mentally sick. The retreat was located outside of the city in the open countryside, and although some form of restraint remained necessary it was kept to the minimum: gone were the chains and manacles. Locks on doors were encased in leather, bars on windows were made to look like window frames, and the walls around the extensive gardens were sunken to make them hardly visible. Occasionally, the employment of a straitjacket was necessary, but this would only have been used as a last resort.

At first the methods employed by the retreat were met with scorn and widespread condemnation, and William felt that he had been deserted by all men. Over time, however, the critics were won over and the retreat became a model which was copied throughout the world. After the death of William, his son Henry Tuke (who had also been a co-founder of the retreat) and his grandson Samuel Tuke continued his work.

FAIRFAX HOUSE

Regarded as the finest Georgian townhouse in England, Fairfax House was built in 1762 for the 9th Viscount Fairfax and it is located in the heart of this stupendous city. The house's stunning interior is an exquisite masterpiece by the famous 18th-century architect John Carr

Fairfax House.

The ancient Shambles.

(1723–1807). Today the house is the home of the renowned Noel Terry collection of English Georgian furniture and clocks. Part of the building was once used as a cinema, from 1921 to 1970. After falling into disrepair the house was finally restored to its former glory by the York Civic Trust in the early 1980s.

MANSION HOUSE

The Mansion House was built in 1735 as the official residence of the Lord Mayor of York. It would be another 20 years before London would follow York's example and build a specific residence for their Lord Mayor. Mansion House was originally constructed because Sir William Robinson, who had been the Lord Mayor at the beginning of the 18th century, had refused to surrender the Red House. This had been built by the architect William Etty in 1702, and it had been the intention of the City Corporation to use this property as the official residence. When Sir William refused to relinquish the house, they were forced into having another house built.

The first royal visitor to Mansion House was Edward Augustus (1739–1767), 10th Duke of York. He was the younger brother of George III, and was the first duke to receive the freedom of the city in 1761.

THE SHAMBLES

Undoubtedly the most famous mediaeval street in York is the Shambles. This ancient narrow thoroughfare has the distinction of being the only existing street in the city which was named in the *Domesday Book*. The majority of the buildings which line this historic street date from the 15th to the 17th century. The name Shambles is derived from 'Shammel' benches, which were used to display meat during the Middle Ages, as this was a street of butchers. It would have once been extremely unpleasant due to its poor sanitation and open sewer, which ran down the centre of the street. Located behind many of the

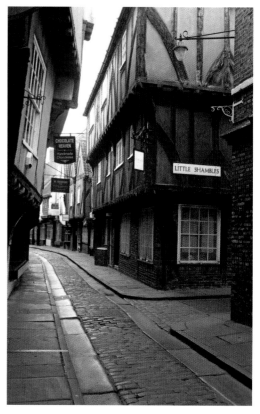

houses were slaughterhouses, and it would have been a common sight to see offal and entrails from the slaughtered animals flung into the streets. It is from this that we would now describe something that is a mess as being a shambles. Originally, the street was called 'Fleshammels', which is an Anglo-Saxon word that means, literally, 'flesh-shelves'.

By the end of the 19th century there were 25 butchers still trading in the Shambles; today, however, there are none. Yet evidence of former times remains, for many of the shops still retain meat hooks outside and shelves, which once displayed the meat.

ROWNTREE'S

In 1862 Henry Isaac Rowntree, who had been working for Tuke and Co., founded Rowntree's when he bought the cocoa and chocolate department from his former employers. Seven years later he was joined by his brother Joseph Rowntree, who would eventually take control of the business when Henry died in 1883.

Joseph was a Quaker and a philanthropist, and would introduce many progressive ideas into the company, including one of the first occupational pension schemes for his employees. Although he was a powerful businessman, he was to remain strongly committed to improving the life of others. As a teenager he had accompanied his father on a trip to Ireland, where he had witnessed the effects of the potato famine. This profound experience would play a significant part in his later political and social views.

He created four Rowntree trusts, which were funded by legacies left by both himself and his son, Benjamin Seebohm Rowntree. These trusts are the Joseph Rowntree Charitable Trust, the Joseph Rowntree Foundation, the Joseph Rowntree Housing Trust, and the Joseph Rowntree Reform Trust: and they are still going to this day. The housing trust owns and manages the model village of New Earswick. This community was created in 1901 when Joseph bought 150 acres of agricultural land and built workers' cottages, a school, a surgery and a folk hall. The village was designed by Barry Parker and Sir Raymond Unwin in the Arts and Crafts movement style. Initially it had been planned that all the religious groups should worship under one roof – the folk hall. However, this proved impractical and in 1914 the Anglican church of St Andrew's was built. Later a Methodist chapel and a meeting house for the Society of Friends were added to the village.

In 1862 Joseph married Julia Eliza Seebohm, but she died a year later. He later married her cousin, Emma Antoinette Seebohm, with whom he had six children. The famous social investigator Benjamin Seebohm Rowntree (often known as Seebohm Rowntree) was their third child and was born in York on 7 July 1871. Seebohm became the chairman of Rowntree's in 1923, a position he would hold until 1941. Joseph died on 24 February 1925 and a plaque on a wall which surrounds the grounds of the retreat informs us that he is buried in the Quaker cemetery within.

By the end of the 19th century Rowntree's had grown from employing 30 people to having a workforce of over 4,000. In 1969 the company merged with its rival Mackintosh to become Rowntree Mackintosh. After going public in 1987 the company was the subject of a takeover battle between Jacobs Suchard and Nestlé in 1988, with Nestlé eventually winning control.

THE VALE OF YORK

THE VALE OF YORK

The Vale of York is a relatively flat swathe of land, which neatly dissects the county of North Yorkshire and separates the Yorkshire Dales on the west from the North Yorkshire Moors and coastline on the east. It stretches from the furthest northern point to the most southerly tip of the county and its flatness has meant that it has been the most logical route for travellers venturing between Scotland and the south of England. This has also resulted in it being the battleground for many a conflict and its soil has been soaked red with the blood of many a fallen soldier. Standing at the various battlefields one is immediately struck by the flatness of the land, and the dreadful realisation that the combatants would have had nowhere to hide.

NORTHALLERTON

There is plenty of evidence to suggest that there has been a settlement at Northallerton since at least Roman times. Situated close to a Roman road, it is thought that it was once a Roman military garrison. Archaeological excavations have unearthed findings which give credence to this belief. On Castle Hill, which can be found just west of the town, there is evidence that the Romans had a signal station.

In 855 a stone church was built at Northallerton. This was to replace an earlier wooden building that had been founded by St Paulinus. Nothing, however, remains of this earlier church. During Saxon times the settlement was known as Alvertune and according to the 13th-century English historian and chronicler Pierre de Langtoft (an Augustinian monk from Bridlington Priory) Northallerton had been the scene of a number of battles between King Elfrid, his brother Alfred and five Danish kings.

The origins of the town's name are not known; however, there are a number of theories, including that it was derived from the 'farm belonging to Aelfere' or possibly King Alfred. It has even been suggested that it simply refers to alder trees, which once grew nearby. We do know, however, that the prefix of North was added in the 12th century and this was to distinguish it from the parish of Allerton Maulever.

Due to its position on a major route, Northallerton has been the scene of conflict on many occasions. On 22 August 1138 English forces, which had been summoned by Archbishop Thurston of York, gathered two miles north of Northallerton at Cowton Moor to repel a Scottish army. The Scottish army was led by King David I of Scotland, who had crossed the border in support of his niece, Empress Matilda, in her claim for the English throne. Many believed her to be the rightful heiress to the throne and viewed King Stephen as a usurper. Stephen was involved with fighting rebel barons in the south, and the Scottish armies, quick to take advantage of this, captured Cumberland and Northumberland, as well as Carlisle and Bamburgh castle.

Early on that August morning the English forces gathered around their standard, which was a ship's mast that had been mounted on a cart. The mast bore a pyx (a small box or container containing a consecrated host) and the banners of the minsters of York, Beverley and Ripon. It was from this that the battle took its name – the Battle of the Standard. Stephen was unable to send a great force to meet the threat in the north and was only able to muster a small number of troops (which mainly consisted of mercenaries). Without an adequate army to face the invaders, it was left to the north to raise the men. Archbishop Thurston worked

This cemetery in Northallerton was once where a castle stood.

tirelessly to this aim and preached that to fight the Scottish was to do God's work.

As the Scottish army arrived at the field of battle they discovered that the English force had already taken up strong defensive positions. Undaunted, King David commanded that his soldiers take up battle formations, which consisted of four lines. Although the English had a better position, he relied on his superiority of numbers. However, this proved to be a costly error and numerous attacks failed under the withering fire of the English archers. A final desperate attack by mounted knights met with some brief success, and could have possibly changed the course of the battle, but it was doomed to failure due to lack of infantry support. When David's reserves deserted him, the die was cast and he conceded defeat, withdrawing from the battlefield. The English forces made a half-hearted attempt to give chase to the fleeing

Scots, but soon gave up the pursuit. David was allowed to fall back to Carlisle, where he regrouped his army. Before a month had passed a truce had been negotiated and, although David had lost the battle, the terms proved very favourable for him, and the north of England was safe once again.

In 1130 a castle was built on the west side of Northallerton by Bishop Rufus, which was expanded by William Cumin in 1142. Bishop Hugh Du Puiset (Hugh Pudsey) further enlarged the castle in 1173. Hugh was a nephew of King Stephen and was the most princely of all the Prince Bishops of Durham. He had formerly been the Treasurer of York and Archdeacon of Winchester. He was a powerful man, who at the time was virtually the ruler of the North of England. After enlarging the castle he had it garrisoned with a group of Flemish soldiers. Enraged by this act, Henry II had the castle destroyed. Twenty years later a fortified

These are the fields upon which the Battle of the Standard was fought on 22 August 1138, between the armies of England and Scotland.

palace was built on the same site. This was a more substantial building complete with a moat, and was to become an important centre of administration for the bishops in Yorkshire as well as a major residence for them. It was also a popular stopping place for royalty and other dignitaries due to Northallerton's location on the main road between York and Durham. Sadly, by 1658 the palace had fallen into a ruinous state and today the site is a cemetery.

In 2006, during development of a site which had once been a Carmelite Priory, archaeologists unearthed the remains of eight monks, together with a selection of artefacts. The priory had been founded in 1354, but was destroyed shortly after the Dissolution of the Monasteries. Over the centuries the land passed through various hands and in 1857 a workhouse was built there. In 1939 Friarage Hospital was opened on the site as an emergency medical centre in the event of bombing raids on Teesside. Between 1943 and 1947 it was commandeered by the military and was a hospital for the RAF. Today it serves a rural population of 122,000 people and an area of 1,000 square miles.

In 1200 Northallerton became a market town by royal charter and to this day a market is still held in the town. Over the centuries the town has been an important centre for trade and transport. It was also an important resting point for travellers. During the heyday of coaching the town possessed four coaching inns. Northallerton once had an important cattle market and drovers would bring cattle, horses and sheep from as far away as Scotland to trade in the town. Originally, the cattle market was held by the church; however, the sheep were sold on the High Street, a practice that was to continue until the early 20th century. There is still a regular livestock market in the town and although it is a lively market town, Northallerton retains its rural ambience. From the 17th century Northallerton held the quarter sessions for the area. Prior to the construction of the Court House in 1875, these were held in a variety of buildings, including the Tollbooth, Guildhall and Vine House. Northallerton is the location of the County Hall headquarters of the North Yorkshire County Council.

OSMOTHERLEY

According to legend, King Osmund of Northumbria was told by a soothsayer that his young son, Oswy, would drown before his third birthday. The king ordered that the queen should take their son to the highest point (Roseberry Topping) and live at the hermitage at the summit until his third birthday had passed. While at the hermitage the young prince drowned in a spring, which flowed from the top of the hill. So distraught was the queen that she died a short time later from grief. The king buried his queen next to their son at a place that was to become known as Oswy-by-his-mother-lay or Osmotherley.

Unfortunately, the origin of the village's name is undoubtedly more prosaic, for 'ley' is the Saxon word for a field or clearing. It is, therefore, much more likely that the name was derived from the first person who owned the land; presumably a man called Osmund. The village is certainly ancient and there is a reference to it in the *Domesday Book*, where it is referred to as Asmundrelac (which interestingly derives from Old Norse and not Saxon).

In the mid-18th century John Wesley was to visit the village on a number of occasions, where he would preach while standing on the barter table. The stone barter table stands near to the village cross and was where goods for sale would be displayed and sold. John Wesley, who was a rather short man, used this table to stand on while preaching in the open air. In 1754 a Methodist Chapel was erected in the village, and it is thought to be the oldest in the world.

In the village stands a stone building, which was erected at the beginning of the 18th century, and is the Osmotherley Friends' Meeting House. It is said that George Fox, the founder of the Society of Friends, may have visited the village in the late 17th century. The Society of Friends is also known as the Quakers; a name first coined in 1650 when George Fox, after being charged with blasphemy, was brought before Judge Bennet of Derby. Fox was later to write in his diary that Bennet had 'called us Quakers because we bid them tremble at the word of God'.

MOUNT GRACE PRIORY

The Mount Grace Priory was founded in 1398 by Thomas Holland, 1st Duke of Surrey and son of Richard II's half-brother Thomas, 2nd Earl of Kent. Thomas Holland was executed on 7 January 1400 after the failed 'Epiphany Rising', which had intended to kill Henry IV and restore Richard II to the throne. After the plot failed it became apparent to Henry IV that it was too dangerous to leave the deposed king alive. So, when on 17 February 1400 Richard met his death under mysterious circumstances in Pontefract Castle, there could be little doubt as to who had had a hand in it.

The priory was the last to be established in Yorkshire, and belonged to the strict Carthusian Order, whose monks live as hermits in their own separate cells, spending their time in silence and solitude. They do not engage in any work of a pastoral or missionary nature, but spend their time in prayer for the salvation of the human race. At various times throughout the week they meet briefly with each other and once a year a member of their family may visit them. The order is also known as the Order of St Bruno and their motto is *Stat crux dum volvitur orbis* meaning 'the Cross is steady while the world is turning'.

In 1410 the rector of Mount Grace Priory, Nicholas Love, completed his English translation of *Meditationes Vitae Christi* (a book which has been attributed to St Bonaventure). Love entitled his translation *The Mirror of the Blessed Life of Jesus Christ*. Under new strictures imposed by the Lambeth Constitutions of 1407–09, any new translation of Biblical material must be submitted to the local bishop for approval. This ruling had been brought about in an attempt to prevent the circulation of the heretic John Wycliffe's English translation of the Bible and other equally dangerous writings (as viewed by the Church).

Conforming to these strictures, Love submitted his manuscript to Thomas Arundel, Archbishop of Canterbury, for approval. His translation included a number of major additions to the original Latin text, additions which were guaranteed to curry favour with the archbishop, who argued fervently against Wycliffe. This was a clever political move, for combined with granting the archbishop confraternity in the spiritual matters of the priory, he was to ensure the provision of material benefits for Mount Grace. This was especially important after the loss of the founder and benefactor, Thomas Holland.

After the Dissolution of the Monasteries the priory fell into a ruinous state, but in the 17th century a manor house was incorporated into the old guesthouse. At the beginning of the 20th century a larger house was constructed in the Arts and Crafts style. Today, Mount Grace Priory is under the care of English Heritage.

THIRSK

In the *Domesday Book* the town is recorded as being called Tresche, which is derived from the Old Norse word firesk, meaning 'marsh'. Thirsk is built around a very large cobbled mediaeval market square, which is surrounded by old houses, shops and inns. At its centre stands an unusual clock tower and bull ring (see Askrigg).

Thirsk once had a castle, which was built in the 11th century by Robert de Mowbray. Robert had been the Earl of Northumbria from 1086, but was deposed in 1095 after rebelling against

The unusual clock tower in Thirsk Market Square.

William Rufus (William II). The castle was later torn down in the late 12th century by Henry II after a failed rebellion led by his sons.

Thomas Lord was born in Thirsk on 23 November 1755. His father had been reduced to labouring after losing his lands for supporting the Jacobite Rising in 1745. While Thomas was still young the family moved to Diss in Norfolk. As a young man Thomas moved to London, where he got a job as a bowler and groundsman at the White Conduit Club, and he later worked as head groundsman for the Earl of Winchester. In 1786 he was encouraged by George Finch, 9th Earl of Winchilsea, and Charles Lennox to start his own private cricket ground. In May 1787 he acquired some land off Dorset Square in London and after the lease on this ground expired in 1810 he moved to new grounds, but these were requisitioned by Parliament in 1813 for the Regent's Canal. He was, therefore, forced to find a third new ground, and in 1814 he moved to the present site, which still bears his name today: Lord's.

On Ingramgate in Thirsk stands a unique old milestone, which shows the figure of a man with a stick in one hand and a tankard of beer in the

Thirsk Hall: since 1723 this building has been the home of the lord of the manor. In 1774 it was extended by the architect John Carr.

This building was once the childhood home of Thomas Lord, who was born here on 23 November 1755. He was to found the Lord's cricket ground. Today this house is a museum.

other. One local tale says that it is to commemorate an old man, who would walk miles each day into Thirsk to have a drink at his favourite inn. However, it is more probable that the figure represents a drover: during the 19th century the driving of cattle from Scotland and the north would reach its peak when a million or more beasts a year would be driven along the ancient drovers' road. Thirsk would have been popular among the drovers, for as well as being an important market there were a number of inns.

Just off the square is the house where the vet James Alf Wight OBE (more commonly known as Alf Wight) once had his practice. He is perhaps better known as the author of a series of books about a fictional country vet – James Herriot. Alf was born in Sunderland on 3 October 1916 and, after qualifying as a vet from Glasgow Veterinary College at the age of 23, he briefly returned to his birthplace to work at a veterinary practice before moving to Thirsk.

For many years he had promised to write a book, but had always put it off, never really finding the time. It was his wife Joan who

provided him with the impetus, for when he was 50 she finally challenged him to write one. After a few false starts and a number of rejections he realised that he should write about something he knew, and the James Herriot stories were the result. They did not prove to be

The unusual milestone which can be found at Ingramgate in Thirsk.

an overnight success and when the first volume was published in 1969 as *If Only They Could Talk* sales were slow at first. After receiving a copy, a New York publisher called Thomas McCormack arranged to have the first two books published as one volume, which he called *All Creatures Great and Small.* The adventures of the country vet soon caught the public's imagination and became a huge success.

BOROUGHBRIDGE

During the Middle Ages the small town of Boroughbridge was a parliamentary borough, and elected two Members of Parliament. It had a 'burgage' franchise until it was abolished in the Reform Act of 1832: this meant that the right to vote had been tied to the ownership of certain properties.

The town was also the scene of a battle, which was fought on 16 March 1322 between Edward II and a number of rebellious barons. The Battle of Boroughbridge resulted in a victory for the king and the leader of the rebels, Thomas, Earl of Lancaster, was executed. Until

This monumental fountain was once where the townsfolk of Boroughbridge obtained their water.

that time the earl had possibly been, with the exception of the king, the most powerful man in the kingdom, and the victory assured the king's position for the next five years. The battle had been a significant advancement in the strategies of warfare, with an emphasis on foot soldiers and a greater reliance on the longbow, rather than the cavalry, which had previously been the mainstay on the battlefield.

In the 18th century Boroughbridge became important as a staging post for coaches travelling between London and Edinburgh. In 1945, while an 80-ton steel mill roll housing was being transported from Sheffield to Falkirk, its incredible weight caused the bridge in the town to collapse. The army installed a temporary Bailey bridge over the River Ure while repairs were undertaken.

THE DEVIL'S ARROWS

The Devil's Arrows are three standing stones which were erected way back in the mists of time. These types of standing stones are known as menhirs, a name which was adopted by 19th century archaeologists. It is formed from two Breton words – 'men' meaning stone and 'hir' meaning long – 'long stone'. Originally, they were thought to have been either late Neolithic or early Bronze Age, and they have long been associated with the Beaker people. Recent evidence, however, suggests that they may be even older. Menhirs can be found in Europe, Africa and Asia; however, they appear to be more prevalent in Western Europe, with the greatest number of examples being in Great Britain, Ireland and Brittany.

The true purpose of these stones remains a mystery, and we can only speculate as to their function. Over the years a number of theories have been put forward; from Druids' stones to ancient boundary markers. One thing which can be certain is that they predate the Druids. We know very little about the people who erected them. With the exception of the

The Devil's Arrows.

menhirs, the occasional finds of shards of pottery, stone tools and jewellery, nothing is known about their social organisation or beliefs – what they thought or even how they spoke.

It is interesting to note that although the sizes of the menhirs vary considerably, their shape is often very similar, in that they tend to taper towards the top. The tallest menhir in the United Kingdom is the Rudston Monolith, which can be found in the grounds of Rudston Parish Church of All Saints, East Yorkshire. This monolith is made from Moor Grit Conglomerate, which was originally brought from the Cleveland Hills near Whitby. In the late 1700s Sir William Strickland carried out archaeological excavations at the stone and discovered that there was as much of it hidden beneath the ground as was standing visibly above. He also unearthed many skulls during his dig, which led him to draw the conclusion that this must have been a sacrificial site.

In 13th-century Sweden, menhirs were still being erected as markers for dead warriors, and Snorri Sturluson wrote in his saga *Heimskringla* that in the earliest age, which was called the Age of Burning, the dead were consumed by fire, and Standing Stones were placed over their ashes. He tells us that this was a custom which remained long after Odin's time.

It is thought that there were originally five Devil's Arrows. One was displaced in the 1700s

The third Devil's Arrow can be found among the trees.

during a failed treasure hunt and was later used in the construction of a local bridge, while the fate of the fourth stone is not told. It appears that these stones were erected in alignment with the southernmost summer moonrise, and are connected with the great ancient complex of Thornborough Henge. They get their name from a legend which dates back to 1721 and states that the Devil threw these stones at Aldborough, but that they fell short. The stones are also known as the Three Sisters and the Three Greyhounds.

The tallest of the stones is 22 feet and 6 inches tall, which makes it the second tallest in the United Kingdom. The stones have distinctive grooves which have been created by rainfall over the millennia. They are composed of millstone grit, and are thought to have been brought from an area near Knaresborough, which is nine miles away.

We may never know why ancient people went to such great lengths to move and erect these fantastic monuments. Perhaps their secrets have now been lost forever over the passage of time and will remain a mystery which can never be solved. But this does not detract from nor diminish the power with which these stones stir our imagination.

ALDBOROUGH AND THE ROMAN TOWN OF ISURIUM

The ancient village of Aldborough was once an important Roman garrison town called Isurium Brigantium. It was the capital of the Brigantes, who were the largest Celtic tribe in Britain. In AD71 Petillius Cerialis, who was at that time the governor of Roman Britain, launched an attack from his base at York. The purpose of this assault was to subjugate the belligerent people of the North and bring them firmly under Roman control. After successfully achieving his goal, he established a new administration centre at Aldborough. Initially a fort, the majority of the settlement would have been made up of

military personnel manning the garrison, with a small number of civilians living around the perimeter.

It is thought that Aldborough may have been the base for the famous Ninth Legion (Legio IX Hispana). This legion had been raised in Spain by Pompey in 65BC. In 61BC they were commanded by Julius Caesar while he was Governor of Further Spain, and they would later remain faithful to him during the civil war. After his victory he disbanded the Ninth, but following his assassination they were recalled by Octavian.

By the early second century military operations at Aldborough were greatly scaled down, and the garrison was replaced by a new civilian centre. At the beginning of the third century a sturdy wall was built around the settlement. This would have been a considerable structure and stood twelve feet tall and nine feet wide at its thickest point. Towers and clay ramparts were erected at intervals along the wall, and the defences were completed

This column is thought to be a memorial to the Battle of Boroughbridge, which was fought on 16 March 1322, and it now stands next to the church in Aldborough.

BYLAND ABBEY

In 1134 a number of monks set out from Furness Abbey; their mission was to found a new abbey. They were to contemplate a number of locations before finally settling on a site near the village of Coxwold. Byland Abbey was originally founded as a Savigniac house. The Savigniac monastic order was founded in the forest of Savigny, Normandy, in 1105 by Vitalis de Martain, who had established a hermitage. The order followed the Rule of St Benedict and wore gowns of grey and white, and they also followed strict rules of fasting combined with heavy manual labour. In 1147 the order was to experience severe financial and administrative problems, which proved too grave for them to continue without help. Therefore, the head of the Savigniac Order, Abbot Serlo of Savigny, approached the General Chapter of Cîteaux for help. It was agreed that the Cistercians would absorb the failing Savigniacs into their order. Following this absorption, Byland became a Cistercian abbey.

The abbey church at Byland was one of the largest and most impressive Cistercian churches in Europe. By the late 12th century Byland and its neighbours Fountains Abbey and Rievaulx Abbey were described as the 'three shining lights of the North'. The architecture of Byland is Early Gothic, and even though little now remains of this once magnificent abbey, one cannot fail to be impressed by its size and obvious grandeur. During excavations beautiful mediaeval floor tiles were uncovered in the church, while the cloisters, which are among the largest in England, were glazed in the 15th century to keep out the cold. The abbey's altar is now at Ampleforth Abbey.

Even though this stupendous 12th-century abbey, with its impressive church, was renowned throughout Cistercian Europe, it would not achieve the financial success or the celebrity of its neighbour, Rievaulx. Although throughout the Middle Ages Byland was to be well known for its sheep rearing and export of wool, the

The site of the old courthouse in Aldborough: the blue plaque commemorates the brave aircrew, who managed to keep their stricken aeroplane flying long enough to avoid the village and consequently saved civilian lives.

by digging a large ditch around the perimeter. There can be no doubt that this was a formidable defence, which could have withstood attack from all but the most determined foe. Two centuries later the ditches were moved further away from the walls so that bastions (semi-circular towers) could be erected.

The name Aldborough is derived from the Anglo-Saxon words 'Ald' and 'burh', meaning old or disused stronghold. Near the church stands an unusual column, which is thought to commemorate the Battle of Boroughbridge 1332.

On the village green, outside where the old Court House once stood, stands a set of double stocks. There is also a plaque nearby which pays tribute to the memory of the brave aircrew of a Lancaster bomber, which caught fire during a training flight. The pilot skilfully manoeuvred the stricken aeroplane so as to miss the village and thus avoid civilian casualties. Sadly, all the crew perished when the Lancaster crashed on nearby Studforth Hill.

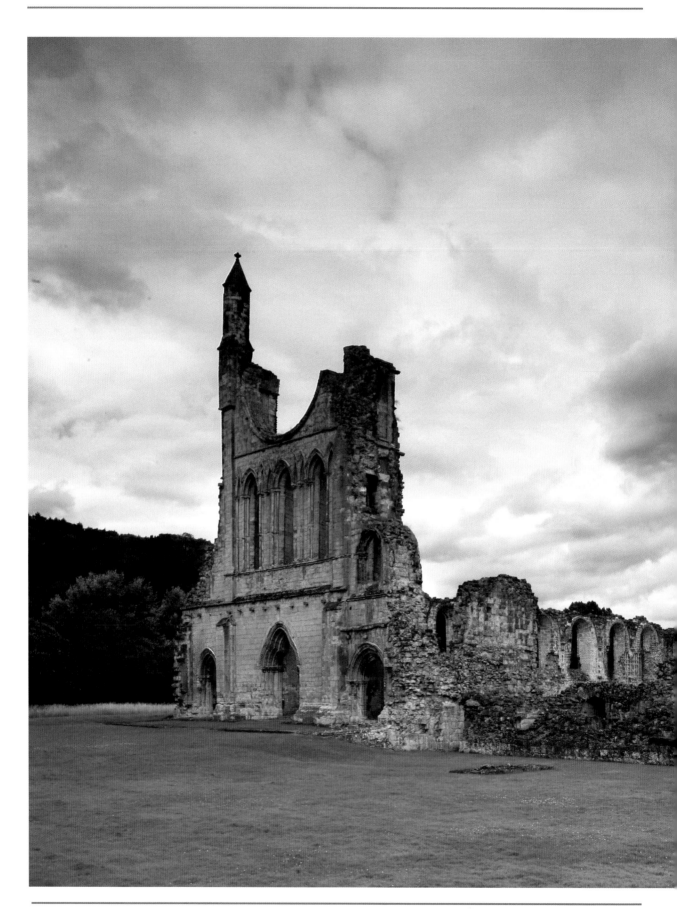

Byland Abbey.

community would experience mixed fortunes. A number of these were self-inflicted; but others were brought about by external forces such as war, famine and plague.

The abbey was once believed to be the last resting place of Roger de Mowbrey. He was the son of Nigel d'Aubigny, who had been one of Henry I's leading men, and Gundreda de Gournay. As a young man, Roger had fought at the Battle of the Standard, where according to accounts of the time he had acquitted himself honourably in the fight against the Scottish army. Roger's reputation for prowess on the battlefield was soon to grow and during the Second Crusade his fame was to increase even further after he defeated a Muslim in one-to-one combat.

It was while on this crusade that Roger was able to rebuild his fortune, which had suffered during the disastrous years of King Stephen's reign. Unfortunately, he was soon to lose it all again after his ill-conceived support of a rebellion against Henry II in 1173–74, which had been led by two of the king's sons, Henry and Richard. In 1186 Roger, who by this time was in his 60s, set off once more to Palestine. He was never to return to England alive, for he was taken captive during the Battle of Hattin in 1187 and died shortly afterwards. His body was buried in the Holy Land.

In the 13th century, however, rumours began to spread among the monks of Byland that Roger was buried beneath the chapter house. In the 16th century the flames of this rumour were fanned by a document from the Augustinian abbey at Newburgh, which Roger had founded. It told a fantastic tale of the life of Roger as an intrepid adventurer and warrior, but it also repeated the rumour which had been started by the monks three centuries earlier. According to the narrative, he did not die while a captive in Palestine, but returned to England very much alive and survived another 15 years. It goes on to say that when he eventually died, his body

was laid to rest beneath the chapter house at Byland. In 1535 the royal commissioners, Doctor Layton and Doctor Legh, during their inspection of the religious houses throughout the north of England, noted that they had seen the sepulchre of Roger and his wife in the chapter house.

In the 19th century a search was undertaken to discover the existence of Roger's grave and a tombstone was found which appeared to give the tale some credence. However, what was thought to be a sword carved on the slab was in fact a mitre, and it is now believed to be the gravestone of a former abbot and not that of this famous warrior. In the 1920s another gravestone was discovered, which did have a sword engraved upon it. It is thought, however, that this stone did not originate from the chapter house, but was simply flung out of the church during the ransacking of the abbey during the 16th century.

It is doubtful that we will ever know the definitive answer, but perhaps a recent theory may go some way towards clearing the mist that shrouds this mystery. According to Gilyard-Beer, the monks of Byland may have felt that it was important that they should have the grave of their founder within the grounds of the abbey, but as this was not possible, they simply built a memorial to him. By the 16th century what had been intended as simply a cenotaph for Roger de Mowbray had been distorted into being his actual place of burial. However, according to this 16th-century narrative he was also supposed to have wrestled with a dragon, so it appears that the document should be taken with a very large pinch of salt.

COXWOLD AND SHANDY HALL

Since at least 700 there has been a church at the same site in the village of Coxwold. The present church was built in 1420, and is dedicated to St Michael. It has an unusual octagonal west

Shandy Hall: once the home of Laurence Sterne.

tower, and the wooden ceiling of the church's interior has a number of interesting bosses, which consist of colourful figures.

From 1760 until his death in 1768, the author Laurence Sterne was the vicar of Coxwold. He lived in the vicarage, which he renamed Shandy Hall after his anti-novel *The Life and Opinions of Tristram Shandy*. According to a stone tablet, which is located over the front door to the house, it was here that Sterne wrote his book. This, however, was not completely true, for he had already published two volumes of his work in 1759 before he took up residency here.

Originally, the parsonage had been built in 1430; however, it was extensively altered in the 17th century, and although Sterne only rented the property from the Fauconberg Estate, he added a number of quirky and eccentric alterations of his own to the building.

An interesting carved face at St Michael's.

One of the wooden bosses found inside St Michael's.

winter. By February 1763 Sterne, however, declared that he had become 'heartily tired of France' and expressed a wish to return home to Yorkshire. It appeared that his wife did not share in his desire and elected to remain in France with their daughter Lydia.

Sterne returned to England where he spent the next few months in London and only returned to his home in Yorkshire in the autumn. When he was back at Shandy Hall he threw himself into his writing and completed a further two volumes of *Tristram Shandy*, which were published in January 1765. In October of that year he set off on a seven-month journey through France and Italy, which he would later write about in his second novel *A Sentimental Journey through France and Italy*, which would be published in the year of his death. He wrote this under the pen name Mr Yorrick.

By the end of the next year he was in London again, and it was here that he met and fell in love with Mrs Eliza Draper, the wife of a Bombay official. Sterne's married life had never been a happy one and he had previously had a number of affairs, including with a French singer called Catherine Fourmantelle and a maidservant. Mrs Draper's husband got wind of the affair and he hastily summoned her back to Bombay. Sterne was smitten and declared his undying love to her; he carried a portrait of her around his neck and sent copies of his books to her. All this, however, did not stop him flirting with other ladies while he was staying in London.

It had been his philandering ways which had initially led to his wife Elizabeth having a nervous breakdown in 1758. After returning to Yorkshire he was joined by his wife and daughter in August 1767, but they soon found each other's company intolerable and it was agreed that she should go back to France with Lydia and he would stay in England. She never returned to England, and although Sterne was happy with this arrangement, he genuinely missed his daughter.

According to Sterne, he spent a wonderful time at Coxwold and stated that while there he was as happy as a prince. This, however, did not prevent him from travelling about. He had been suffering from ill-health and since his last year at college in 1736 had been constantly struggling against the effects of consumption.

In January 1762 he obtained a year's leave of absence from the Archbishop of York and set off for Paris. He planned to journey to the South of France as the weather would be more beneficial to his damaged lungs, as the previous year he had suffered a severe haemorrhage of the lungs. This began a journey through France and Italy, where the Sterne family would make their home for a period before once again travelling to a new destination. After travelling through the Pyrenees, they eventually settled in Marseilles in September 1763, where they stayed through the

In 1768, while visiting his London publisher, he became ill with influenza and on 18 March he died. Two days after his burial in a graveyard near the Bayswater Road in London, bodysnatchers dug up his corpse and sold it for research. The body's identity was discovered during a lecture at Cambridge and the dissection was immediately stopped, but not before the lecturer had sawn off the top of the skull. Sterne's body was reburied.

In 1969 the Laurence Sterne Trust learnt that the graveyard where he was buried had been sold to developers and plans had been approved to build flats upon it. They were galvanised into immediate action and sought permission to exhume the author's body and rebury it at Coxwold. However, when the grave was opened they were faced with a conundrum for it contained five skulls, but as one of them had had its top removed this narrowed down their choices somewhat. Further examination of the skull by taking measurements and comparing the results with a bust of Sterne conclusively proved that this was the right one. His remains were brought back to Yorkshire and reburied in the grounds of St Michael's. As a final note to this strange tale, and one which no doubt Sterne himself would be amused by, he has two gravestones.

THORNBOROUGH HENGE

The ancient monument of Thornborough Henge is known to be 1,000 years older than the pyramids of Giza. This epic site is one mile long and the size of 12 Stonehenges. The magnificent complex is made up of three circular earthworks with ditches and banks and was built in alignment with the rising of the constellation of Orion, which happens each autumn. The positioning of the circles would, therefore, have had great significance to the pagan worshippers and their accuracy was, by any standards, a monumental achievement in civil engineering. More so, considering the instruments which are now available to the modern engineer, such as the theodolite. This would, indeed, have been a very sacred place for our distant forefathers.

It is the largest ritual religious site in the British Isles and the construction of these 5,500-year-old earthworks would have been a fantastic feat, for it would have easily taken many millions of man-hours to complete. Originally, the henge would have been covered with white gypsum, which would have presented an awesome sight to these prehistoric inhabitants. It would be no exaggeration to state that this ancient monument should be regarded as not only one of the major man-made achievements in Britain, but perhaps also throughout the whole of Europe.

SHERIFF HUTTON

The ancient village of Sheriff Hutton is so called because it was once held by Bertram de Bulmer, who was the Sheriff of York. The Bulmers were an ancient family, who it is said were aristocrats of Anglo-Saxon origin and who had remarkably kept their status after the Norman Conquest. The name means bull mere (a lake frequented by a bull) and is derived from the Gaelic – 'Búir na mara'. It is, therefore, more than possible that the family could trace its roots as far back as the Brigantes, who lived in the area even before Roman times.

The castle at Sheriff Hutton.

The Church of St Helen and the Holy Cross at Sheriff Hutton: it is thought to be where Richard III's son is buried.

In 1140 Bertram built a motte and bailey castle, the remains of which can still be seen to the south of the churchyard. The village also has the ruins of a stone castle, which was erected in the late 14th century by John Neville, the 3rd Baron Neville de Raby (1328–1388). His great grandson Richard Neville, 16th Earl of Warwick, was known as the 'Kingmaker'. He earned this title after playing an instrumental part in the deposing of two kings – the Lancastrian Henry VI and the Yorkist Edward IV. Richard was born on 22 November 1428, but little is known about the childhood of this powerful man. In the 1450s he emerged into the world of English politics, in which he would take a significant role, first as a supporter of Henry VI. However, he would soon change allegiance after becoming involved in a territorial dispute with Edmund Beaufort, 1st Duke of Somerset.

When Edward IV took the throne Richard initially gave him his support. But relations turned sour over foreign policy and the king's choice of a bride. Richard renewed his support for Henry VI, and played an active part in restoring him to the throne. On 14 April 1471 Richard was killed while attempting to escape from the field of battle. The decisive Battle of Barnet resulted in a victory for the House of York; poor visibility due to fog had led to the Lancastrians attacking their own men in confusion. The battle lasted between three and four hours and left 1,500 men dead, many of them being slain as they tried to flee.

Sheriff Hutton's parish Church of St Helen and the Holy Cross is thought to be the only location outside of London where a Prince of Wales is buried: Richard III's only son Edward of Middleham, who died in 1484. The death of the 11-year-old prince left Richard without an heir, and also presented Henry Tudor with the opportunity to take the throne of England at the Battle of Bosworth Field in 1485. There is some doubt, however, that the young prince is buried at the church.

THE BATTLE OF TOWTON

Today, as one stands next to the simple Celtic cross that is located next to a road that cuts through the open, flat and windswept fields, it is impossible to believe that this was once the scene of an incomparable tragedy. Even the most imaginative would find it difficult to conjure up the sheer horror and sickening fear which would have been felt by the opposing armies of the Houses of Lancaster and York as they faced each other early one Palm Sunday over 600 years ago. Of the approximately 50,000 soldiers on the field of battle that day on 29 March 1461, it is reputed that about 28,000 were slaughtered.

It is said that Henry VI had not wanted to fight, but had wished to respect this holy day; however, the enemy was at hand and his troops were ready to hurl themselves into the fray. The mood in the camp would have been sombre as the men prepared themselves for battle. The only sounds would have been the scrape of cold steel against stone as they sharpened their weapons and quietly reflected; perhaps saying their final prayers and making their peace with their maker. Unable to restrain them any longer, Henry sounded the battle alarm.

It was a miserable day for battle: it was bitterly cold and, as the opposing forces began to move into formation, snow began to fall. The opposing forces raced to reach their chosen ground, which would perhaps give them some advantage over their foe. As the armies marched into position, the Yorkists were outnumbered; however, as the battle began it soon became apparent that the weather conditions had put the Lancastrian forces at a disadvantage, for the snow and wind was blowing into their faces. The commander of the Yorkist vanguard, Lord Falconberg, realising the advantage they had, was quick to capitalise on the good fortune and

ordered his archers to shoot one flight of arrows, which easily hit their mark. Each man would be carrying between 60 and 72 arrows, which could last him from three to six minutes if he maintained a rate of 20 shots per minute, which would have been expected of an experienced archer. But even the most experienced would have found it difficult to maintain this rate of fire over a prolonged period, as the muscles of his shoulders and arms would rapidly become tired and even his fingers would have become strained through the effort.

Falconberg then ordered his archers to hold their ground while the Lancastrian forces fired all their arrows in retaliation. Unfortunately, the Lancastrians were unable to see their enemy due to the falling snow, which effectively blinded them, and as they were firing into a

This cross commemorates the bloodiest battle ever to be fought on British soil: the Battle of Towton.

headwind their arrows did not have the same reach and fell short. Once their quivers were empty, Falconberg commanded his archers, who were unscathed, to march forward firing off their arrows. Not only did the Yorkist archers empty their quivers, but they also gathered the arrows of the Lancastrians, which had fallen short. It is said that this was the largest release of arrows ever to have taken place in the British Isles.

The Lancastrian forces could not withstand this onslaught of arrows raining down on them for much longer, especially the light-armoured archers in the front ranks, who were suffering huge losses from the lethal hail. Soon they were falling back through the ranks in panic, which began to unnerve the other soldiers, and there was an imminent danger of the Lancastrian army breaking ranks and the battle becoming a rout. Aware of this possibility, the Lancastrian commanders ordered the whole force to advance. Seeing the advancing enemy, the Yorkist archers made for the cover of their own ranks, but before doing so they let off a few further volleys of arrows into the packed ranks as a parting shot. The entire Lancastrian army moved with gritted determination towards the Yorkists, who awaited their foe with equal determination. The two armies clashed with such force that a shudder went through the front line of the Yorkists and the line was nearly broken. But it held and what followed was hours of savage combat. Swords, maces and battleaxes slashed and smashed, inflicting hideous and mortal injuries as the death toll mounted. No quarter was asked for and none was given.

With grim determination the opposing forces battled on, resolved either to conquer or die in the field. The deadly conflict continued for 10 hours, and for a time one side would appear to have the upper hand and then the other. The death toll was so great that both sides had to momentarily stop fighting to clear away the bodies that were accumulating so that they could continue with the butchery. It is said that at the height of the battle the Earl of Warwick, who was commanding the Yorkist right flank, dismounted and killed his horse as a sign to his troops that he would stand with them to the bitter end. The battle had been raging for about three hours when, shortly after midday, several hundred Lancastrian troops appeared from Castle Hill Woods where they had been hiding, waiting for the ideal moment to attack their foe. They smashed into the Yorkists' left flank, which caused them to give way to some extent and led to some of the Lancastrian commanders believing that they had won the battle. However, the right and left flanks of the Lancastrian army were not co-ordinated and were fighting separate battles.

By early afternoon the Yorkists began to give ground all along the front and it appeared that perhaps the battle was lost. It was at this point that Edward decided to commit the reserve troops, which he was commanding, into the fight, to shore up the faltering line, prevent it collapsing and stave off disaster. Edward was every inch the figure of a young king and would have presented an impressive figure. Standing a little over six feet tall and in full armour, his presence on the battlefield at this decisive moment would no doubt have boosted the morale of the flagging Yorkist troops. Although committing the reserves would have given the tired troops some hope, it did not reverse the Yorkist fortunes and by 4 o'clock it seemed all over for them. The line was beginning to break and it seemed inevitable that a rout would shortly follow. Suddenly, it seemed that a miracle had happened, for a force of 5,000 men had arrived. The force had been gathered from East Anglia and was led by the Duke of Norfolk. The duke had been ill, which had impeded the progress of his troops, but when they had arrived at Pontefract Castle he learnt that the battle had already commenced. Unable to go any further himself and concerned that the Yorkists would need his troops, he sent them on commanded by his cousin, Sir John Howard.

Although Norfolk's troops would undoubtedly have been tired from their day's march, they were not battle fatigued and their presence was soon to turn the tide of the battle once and for all. The Lancastrian line began to waver and collapse and the arrival of fresh Yorkist troops at this late stage sapped their morale and resolve. By 5 o'clock the whole of the Lancastrian front broke and soldiers in their thousands turned and ran in panic. The slaughter in the rout was appalling and so many died in their attempt to flee that this part of the battlefield is called Bloody Meadow. It is said that the carnage was so great that the rivers Cock and Wharfe ran red with blood. Edward had given orders for his cavalry to pursue the Lancastrians, with instructions to 'kill the lords but spare the commoners', but it appears that his command was ignored and both commoners and nobles were butchered by the victors. This, it appears, may have been revenge for the harsh treatment that the Yorkists had received at the hands of their enemies after previous battles.

So ended the largest, longest and bloodiest battle to be fought on British soil. There is some disagreement about how many perished on that day. The Croyland Chronicle records that 38,000 men died, whereas Edward VI wrote in a letter to his mother that 28,000 died: evidence appears to agree with the latter figure. Whatever the true figure, and it is doubtful that we will ever know for sure, there can be no denying that there is no comparison to the butchery inflicted on that day at Towton.

THE BATTLE OF MARSTON MOOR

On 2 July 1644 the Royalist forces led by Prince Rupert of the Rhine and the Marquess of Newcastle met the Parliamentarian forces led by Sir Thomas Fairfax and the Earl of Manchester on Marston Moor. What would follow was the largest and bloodiest battle of the English Civil War. It would also prove to be a resounding and unequivocal defeat for the Royalists, and would effectively bring an end to their grip on the north of England.

The previous day Prince Rupert had successfully relieved the besieged city of York, and he now stood on Marston Moor in a buoyant mood, impatient to catch the enemy unawares and claim a great victory for the Royalist cause. When he joined him at noon, William Cavendish, the Marquess of Newcastle, was strongly opposed to a pitched battle at this juncture, while Rupert, although supremely confident of a Royalist victory, wished to encounter the enemy before further Parliamentarian reinforcements could increase their number. But Cavendish faced other more pressing problems, for his troops had not been paid and were refusing to fight unless they received their back pay. In addition, a number of his troops were missing and were pillaging the abandoned encampments and trenches outside York. This, combined with the fact that Rupert's own troops were tired from their previous day's long march, led him to finally concede to Cavendish's wishes and delay the attack, with what turned out to be dire consequences.

As the day wore on, the Parliamentarian forces grew stronger as more and more men arrived and strengthened their positions. With the delays it was not until early evening that the Royalists were fully deployed; however, by this time the weather had changed for the worse. Given the conditions, Rupert was persuaded to postpone his attack until the following day. Shortly after 7.30pm a thunderstorm broke and the Royalist troops began to break ranks for their supper: it was at this moment that the Parliamentarian forces received their orders to attack.

The fighting continued in the dark, and of the 17,000-strong Royalist forces 4,000 were killed and 1,500 were taken prisoner. The Parliamentarian force lost only 300 men. In the opening attack Cromwell had received a pistol ball wound to the neck, which had resulted in him temporarily leaving the battlefield to have his wound dressed. He had been given command of the left wing, and along with his troops he had about 800 Scots dragoons. It would be his success on this day which would guarantee his reputation as an outstanding leader. There is, however, some debate about the part he actually played in the final victory at Marston Moor, and some say that the credit should go to Sir Thomas Fairfax or the Scotsman David Leslie, the brilliant strategist who had commanded the Scottish cavalry.

SELBY

Thirteen miles south of York stands the market town of Selby. Once part of the West Riding of Yorkshire, with the enforcement of the Local Government Act it became part of North Yorkshire in 1974. It was the birthplace of Henry I, who was born here in 1069. He was the fourth son of William the Conqueror, and his mother Matilda had been staying at Selby while her husband was 'Harrying the North'.

After his elder brother William II (commonly known as William Rufus; possibly due to his red-faced appearance) was killed while hunting in the New Forest in August 1100, Henry took the throne of England. The circumstances of William's death remain a mystery: he had been killed by a single arrow through his lung…but was it an accident, or was it murder? His body had been left abandoned by the hunting party of nobles, to be found the next day by a group of peasants.

Although this may at face value appear suspicious in itself, it should be remembered that at that time law and order in the realm would die with the king. The nobles would, quite understandably, be looking after their own interests and would hasten back to their estates to make sure that they were secure. According to the chronicler, William of Malmesbury, his death was simply an accident and the result of a wild shot which had missed its intended target – a stag. It was a noble called Walter who fired the fateful shot, and he had attempted to help the mortally wounded king, but it was useless, and, fearing that he might be accused of murder, he took to his horse and fled.

Henry raced to Winchester to secure the royal treasury, and then went on to London, where he was crowned a few days later. His reign, which lasted 35 years, was noted for its judicial and financial reforms, and he became known as Beauclerc for his scholarly interests and also as Lion of Justice.

Another famous character from the pages of history to come from Selby was Robert Aske, born in 1500 and the younger son of Sir Robert Aske of Aughton, near Selby. The family was a leading old Yorkshire family, and had close connections with the Clifford family.

Robert was a lawyer and a Fellow at Gray's Inn, London. He was also a devout Roman Catholic and fiercely objected to Henry VIII's religious reforms. Robert was returning to Yorkshire from London when rebellion broke out in York. Although initially he took no part in the uprising, he soon took up the cause and was to lead it. Robert drew up the demands of the rebels and he gave it its name: the Pilgrimage of Grace.

On 13 October 1536 Robert met with a number of royal delegates to attempt to bring a peaceful end to the rebellion and to be granted an audience with the king. Robert, after receiving their assurances, headed for London for an audience with the king. He received a number of promises of redress from Henry VIII in person, but as he made his journey back north, fighting broke out once more. The king was incensed and

The monument to the Battle of Marston Moor.

The magnificent Selby Abbey.

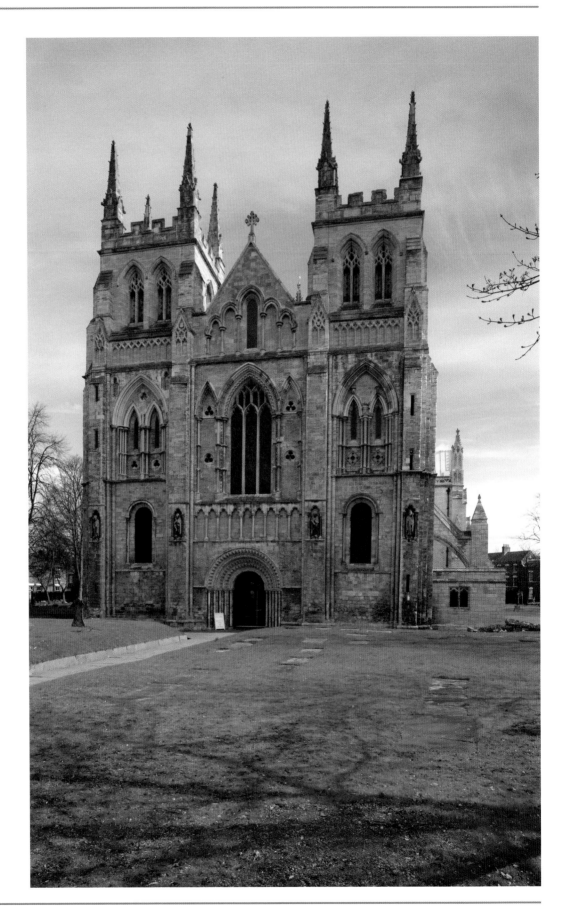

had Robert arrested and brought back to London, where he was sent to the Tower.

Robert was convicted of high treason and sentenced to death. While in the Tower he wrote to the king, begging for mercy and asking to be spared from being hung, drawn and quartered. It is said that he asked if he could be hanged in chains, for he considered this to be the less painful method of execution. This would be a mistake on his part, for being hanged in chains was a very prolonged form of execution, which could take up to six days as the victim slowly suffocated. The king acquiesced and Robert was taken to York, where he was hanged outside Clifford's Tower on 12 July 1537.

SELBY ABBEY

In 1069 an abbey was founded at Selby by a French monk called Benedict. He had come from Auxerre, bringing with him the preserved finger of St Germain. It had been a vision which had prompted him to leave his homeland and to travel to England in search of a place called Selebaie (the Sallow Village). As he arrived at Selby he witnessed three swans landing on the waters of the River Ouse and, taking this as a good omen, he chose this as the site for his new monastery. With permission from William the Conqueror, work began on constructing the Benedictine abbey.

On 31 May 1256 the abbey was conferred with the grant of the mitre. There was only one other 'mitred abbey' in the north of England and that was St Mary's Abbey at York, so this was a great honour which had been bestowed on Selby. The abbot was now permitted to wear the mitre and Papal ring and carry the Papal staff. Although the original grant had been made in perpetuity, after the death of the abbot it was allowed to lapse into disuse for a number of years. On 11 April 1308 Archbishop Grenefield was to reconfirm the grant and Selby would remain a 'mitred abbey' until the Dissolution.

Although by the early 16th century the abbey's fortunes were in decline, at the Dissolution it fared better than many of its contemporaries. This was due in the main to the friendship between the abbot Robert Rogers and Henry VIII. The abbot's name would appear on the petition, which had been signed on 13 July 1530, that favoured the king's divorce. Robert also flatly refused to join the Pilgrimage of Grace. So when the abbey was finally surrendered on 6 December 1539, he was rewarded for his loyalty with a handsome pension of £100 per year, while the monastery's other 23 monks also received generous pensions.

After the Dissolution many of the abbey's buildings were demolished; however, the church remained intact and in 1618, during the reign of James I, it would become Selby's parish church. Although this should have guaranteed its future, it was allowed to fall into decay until, after years of neglect, the central tower collapsed in 1690 and destroyed the south transept. A replacement tower was constructed, but it did not compare with the original and the transept was left unrepaired. In the mid-19th century a major restoration was undertaken by Sir George Gilbert Scott, but in 1906 tragedy struck when a fire broke out and almost destroyed the whole church. Work to restore the building began immediately, and it was down to the determination and optimism of the Reverend Maurice Parkin that this wonderful building did not become another of Yorkshire's ruinous abbeys. Today this beautiful church still stands, proud and majestic, in the centre of Selby.

THE YORKSHIRE DALES

The word 'dale' is derived from the Old Norse word 'dalr', meaning valley, and it is a name which truly befits the Yorkshire Dales, for this rugged landscape is made up of a multitude of valleys – great and small. Many of them are named after the rivers or streams which flow through them. The dales were mainly created by the action of the glaciers that covered the region during the last Ice Age, known as the Devensian Glaciations, which occurred during the latter part of the Pleistocene epoch (which lasted from 1.8 million to 10,000 years ago). The last Ice Age reached its peak about 18,000 years ago.

Although there are only eight major dales, there are literally hundreds of smaller ones, each full of character and steeped in history. In 1954 the Yorkshire Dales National Park was established. It covers an area of 650 square miles and is truly a special place, boasting magnificent scenery and a rich variety of wildlife.

SWALEDALE

As well as being the deepest and narrowest of the dales, Swaledale is also the most northerly. It takes its name from the River Swale, which during the seventh century was used by St Paulinus to baptise many of those whom he had converted. Unlike its neighbour Wensleydale, which has a number of smaller tributary valleys, Swaledale has only one: Arkengarthdale.

ARKENGARTHDALE AND LEAD MINING

Today only a few isolated hamlets and villages remain in Arkengarthdale, but this dale was once the centre of a thriving lead mining industry, with a population running into the thousands.

We cannot be certain when the mining of lead first began. It can, however, be surmised that some form of extraction was undertaken as far back as the Bronze Age, for evidence has shown that early artefacts from this period

Opposite: This waterfall is on Slei Gill, which flows into Arkle Beck. It is from Arkle Beck that Arkengarthdale gets its name. It is said to be named after Arkil, who was a Viking chieftain.

This structure remains from the lead mining industry.

The dramatic Arkengarthdale: it is easy to see how harsh the conditions would have been for the lead miners.

contain small quantities of lead in their composition, and it is believed that this was deliberately added. There can be no doubt that there would have been a lead mining industry during the Roman period as they used this metal for a number of purposes, including roofs, coffins and plumbing. The Roman word for lead is 'plumbum', from which the modern plumber derives his name. Until recently, water pipes were made from lead, and in the past a plumber would not just fix one's plumbing, but would also be responsible for fixing the lead flashing on roofs.

It appears that after the Romans had left the region the industry fell into disuse and it was not until after the Norman Conquest that lead mining was revitalised. There is documentary evidence dating from the 12th century which shows that Jervaulx Abbey held the mining rights to lead and iron ore in Wensleydale. Many of the other monasteries also possessed mining rights to the various dales.

The mining of lead was of great importance to the economy of the dales. It was a highly speculative industry, for although it was possible to extract great quantities the veins were extremely unpredictable and ones which appeared rich in ore could soon prove to be barren. Other ores such as copper and zinc were found side by side with the lead in these mines and sometimes in such quantities as to make their extraction a financially viable proposition. Many of the mines were located deep in the rugged moorlands, miles away from the nearest settlements, and it was unusual to find one in a meadow or enclosed pasture. This meant that not only was the extraction of the ore hard work, but also reaching the mines could only be accomplished by an arduous walk. Often the miners would stay at the mines for days on end.

Most of the mining took place near to or on the surface in small pits, shallow shafts and opencast trenches. The small pits are often erroneously referred to as bell pits, but these

This massive heap of rocks in the valley remains as a natural memorial to the long-abandoned lead mining industry.

types of pits were more commonly used in the mining of coal. The opencast trenches often used a technique called hushing, which had been used as far back as the Romans. This involved damming streams and directing the water into trenches, which would result in the soil and peat being washed away, to hopefully reveal a rich vein of the valuable ore.

The industry reached its peak in 1750 and this lasted until 1850, but by the late 19th century it experienced a rapid decline in the dales. This was mainly due to falling prices as a result of foreign competition. For a brief period Britain had been the world's biggest producer, but by the beginning of the 20th century the veins which had once been so rich in ore had become exhausted, and although the industry was to limp on for a number of years it was inevitable that it would eventually collapse. Many of the companies discovered that they now had worthless mines and their most valuable assets were the buildings and machinery, which they sold for scrap. Miners were left with the proposition of no work, or

Burnt heather on the moorland: the practice of burning the heather ensures that it grows strong and healthy.

they could emigrate to the countries that were still mining lead, such as Germany, Spain and the US, which proved to be a popular destination. Ironically, it had been the British companies which had initially helped the foreign mines set up.

Today the mines have long been abandoned, but the heaps of spoil remain as telltale signs of a once-thriving industry. As one stands looking down through the rugged landscape, one cannot fail to be moved by the thought of the men and women who toiled on this land to extract the soft and malleable metal from the ground.

THE GLORIOUS TWELFTH

It was in the 1850s that the shooting of grouse became popular as a country pursuit for the well-to-do; this was largely due to the opening up of the countryside with a network of railways and the introduction of safer guns. For a number of reasons, this 'sport' generates strong emotions on both sides of the fence: those who strongly oppose it and those who indulge in it. Regardless of the rights and wrongs of this pursuit, there can be no denying the benefits which it has brought to the moorlands of the North in its management and husbandry of the heather. The heather, which left to its own devices becomes sparse and woody, through careful management maintains healthy growth and regeneration of the moorland is ensured. With periodic burning of the heather in controlled areas of 10 to 12-year rotations, a lush blanket of heather can be maintained. This has not only been to the benefit of the grouse, but also to a number of other species, which have been able to thrive due to this careful tending of the land.

After World War One many of the shooting estates were abandoned due to the loss of so many young men in the conflict. A generation decimated – the flower of a nation cut down – followed by a social revolution resulted in many shooting parties becoming a thing of the past.

This has led to many moors becoming derelict and unable to support the great variety of wildlife, which the well-maintained moorland is able to do. For many, however, 12 August still means the official start of the game season.

LANGTHWAITE

The largest settlement in Arkengarthdale is Langthwaite, which derives its name from Old Norse 'langr thveit', meaning a long clearing. It was once famous for its lead mining and according to an unlikely local legend the village provided the roofing materials for Jerusalem in the days of King Herod.

Over the centuries the area has been responsible for the development of many unusual traditions, such as the baking of funeral cakes, which were given to the mourners after the ceremony. These cakes were actually a type of rich shortbread, which was cut into triangles after baking and wrapped in white paper that was sealed with black wax. They were taken to the funeral in a clothes basket.

On 24 September 1817 the foundation stone was laid for a new church, which was paid for by a legacy that had been left by the local lord of the manor, George Brown. The church was to replace the original parish church, which had been located close to Arkle Beck. By the early 19th century this church had become too dangerous to use due to the erosion of the river bank and it was necessary to abandon it. The new church contains the font saved from its predecessor.

St Mary's Church at Langthwaite, in the ancient parish of Arkengarthdale. This church replaced one which was located near Arkle Beck and became too dangerous to use.

The bridge at Langthwaite: this marks the beginning of an arduous walk to Arkengarthdale. This route eventually leads one to the quaintly named hamlet of Booze (which in 1473 was known as Bowehous). Ironically, the hamlet has no public houses.

Today, the region no longer possesses a lead mining industry, but its undeniably beautiful landscape has proved irresistible to many TV and film makers, who have used it as a backdrop for numerous popular productions.

REETH

In Saxon times Reeth was no more than a small settlement on the edge of a forest, but by the 11th century it had grown enough in stature to warrant an entry in the *Domesday Book*. There can be little doubt, though, that there has been some form of settlement here since ancient times, for artefacts were unearthed in the 19th century which date back to the Bronze Age. The quality of the metalwork of these finds is such that we are safe to assume that this area was one of wealth and possibly belonged to the social elite.

Not only did Reeth become an important market town for the local farming community, but it was also to develop into the centre of the region's lead industry. Its close proximity to the lead mines of Arkengarthdale made it an ideal location. It was also to become renowned for hand-knitting, as it was common practice

among the miners to knit while walking to and from the mines. At its peak, the lead industry attracted workers from all over the country, including Cornwall and Wales, and at any one time there were as many as 4,000 employed in

This stone bridge at Reeth was built by the famous 18th-century architect John Carr.

This drinking fountain at the centre of Reeth was presented to the town by George Robinson of Richmond in 1868.

the mines. Locally, as much as 40,000 tons of lead per annum was being extracted from the ground.

On the edge of the village there stands an 18th-century stone bridge, which crosses the River Swale. This was designed by the prolific architect John Carr, whose work can be seen all over Yorkshire and further afield.

KIPLIN HALL

The Jacobean era was a time of rapid advancement in the arts, literature and the sciences. The period ran for the length of James I's reign, from 1603 to 1625. The word is derived from the Hebrew name for James, which is Jacob. It was during this period that William Shakespeare was to write a number of his best-known plays, including *Macbeth*, *King Lear* and what is generally thought to be his last play, *The Tempest*. It was also a time for the sciences and the works of Sir Francis Bacon (1561–1626) would play a crucial part of the evolution of modern science. In 1611 the authorised King James version of the English Bible was published. Although today the copyright on this version of the Bible has expired throughout the world and it is freely printed, in the United Kingdom the rights are still held by the Crown and will continue to be so until 2039.

At the end of the 16th century England was undergoing a change in architecture from the timber-framed buildings of Tudor times to the introduction of Renaissance designs. The Elizabethans were to introduce features such as

St Andrew's Church at Grinton, near Reeth, known by some as the 'Cathedral of the Dale'. For many centuries it was the only parish church in the whole of Swaledale. The oldest part of this magnificent church is Norman; however, there once was an earlier Anglo-Saxon church on this site.

the Dutch gable (a stair-step design at the top of the gable end, also known as 'trapgevel') and Flemish strap-work. The Jacobean builders were to continue with these themes; however, theirs would be a more consistent application of design, adopting Renaissance motifs that rather than being introduced directly from Italy had come through German and Flemish carvers. These Jacobean gabled manor houses were widely regarded as being the epitome of the English country house and the architecture of the period was to have an enduring impact on future buildings. It was an exciting time, which witnessed the introduction of new ideas, such as the use of red brick as a building material. An excellent example can be found at Kiplin Hall at Scorton, near Richmond, which was built in the early 1620s by George Calvert, a local gentleman.

George Calvert was born in 1580 and his father, Leonard, was a country gentleman who had leased some land at Kiplin. It was uneasy

times for the family as Leonard Calvert was a Roman Catholic, and consequently the family found themselves the victims of harassment by the local authorities on more than one occasion. In the same year that George had been born his father had been compelled to promise that he would conform to the State religion, which meant that both he and his family were forced to attend church and abandon their Papist ways. In 1592, however, the family was once again in trouble with the authorities after it had been discovered that one of George's tutors was using a 'Popish primer' to teach the young boy. Leonard was commanded to send both George and his brother, Christopher, to a Protestant tutor, and if necessary they were to present the two children before a board of commissioners once a month to evaluate their progress. He had no option but to obey this demand.

We cannot know how genuine Leonard would have been when making his promises of conformity, but we can assume that like many

The historic Kiplin Hall is located between Richmond and Northallerton. It is an excellent example of the Jacobean country house.

of the gentry who were Roman Catholic and forced to make similar promises his conversion to the Protestant faith would have been insincere and done only to protect his family and maintain a veneer of respectability. There can be no doubt that in private he remained true to his faith and continued with his Catholicism in secret. However, in the case of the Calverts perhaps not secret enough, for in 1593 his second wife, Grace (George's mother had died while he was still an infant), was taken into custody by a 'pursuivant': an official who was responsible for the identification and prosecution of Catholics.

In 1593 George Calvert went to Trinity College, Oxford, where he studied foreign languages. No doubt he would have been compelled to pledge conformity while at university, for it was compulsory for anyone over the age of 16 to swear an oath of allegiance. In 1597 he received his bachelor's degree and moved to London, where he studied law at Lincoln's Inn for three years.

In 1601 he set off on an extended trip to Europe, which was to last until 1603. It was at this time that he became known as a specialist in foreign affairs, and it was also the beginning of an association which was to prove instrumental to his future success. He had met and become friends with Sir Robert Cecil, who was spymaster to Elizabeth I. Sir Robert was to orchestrate the smooth succession of James I to the throne of England. James was keen to reward Sir Robert for his loyalty and promotion was to follow; he soon became the most powerful man at the royal court. This influential man was a good friend to have for the ambitious young Calvert, for as Sir Robert rose, so did George.

With his foreign languages, legal training and discretion he was soon to become a valuable asset to Sir Robert. George had been thrust into the centre of court politics and now found himself acquiring a number of small offices, honours and sinecures. Over time he would continue to grow in power until in 1619 he was appointed Secretary of State – an appointment which would come as a shock to many, but not to Calvert himself. In 1623 James I further rewarded him for his loyalty by granting him a 2,300-acre estate in County Longford, Ireland, which was known as the Manor of Baltimore.

In 1625 he resigned from his position as Secretary of State due, it was said, to ill-health. Shortly after his resignation he announced that he had converted to Catholicism and although many were outwardly surprised at the news, a few hinted that they had had their suspicions. In March of that year the king had suffered from a stroke and a fever, and finally passed away during a violent bout of dysentery: his son Charles was crowned king of England. The new king maintained Calvert's barony and his place on the Privy Council, but by this time Calvert had turned his attention to his Irish estates and his overseas investments. He was also to secure Charles's blessing for a venture in Newfoundland. Five years earlier he had purchased a tract of land in Newfoundland, which he had called Avalon (named after the legendary place where Christianity had been introduced to Britain).

It was clear that he had colonial ambitions, and although Avalon prospered for the first few years, the colony eventually failed due to the harsh conditions. In 1627 he set sail for Virginia, where he had land, but he found that he was not welcome after refusing to take the compulsory oath of allegiance. Two years later he petitioned the king for land that lay in a more congenial climate. In 1632 he died before he could receive his charter for the new colony at Maryland, which was eventually received two months later by his son Cecil. Maryland would develop into the prime tobacco-producing colony in the Mid-Atlantic states and, more importantly, became a refuge for Catholic settlers.

In 1699 Benedict Leonard Calvert, 4th Lord Baltimore, married Lady Charlotte Lee, granddaughter of Charles II by his mistress Barbara Villiers, Duchess of Cleveland. Although it proved not to be a happy marriage, they nevertheless produced seven children. Eleven years later they divorced and caused a scandal throughout the whole of English society. She remarried five years later and her new husband, Christopher Crowe, bought Kiplin Hall from Charles Calvert, 5th Lord Baltimore, for £7,000 in 1722. Christopher began a programme of purchasing land around the estate, which his descendants continued to implement, resulting in the estate eventually exceeding 5,000 acres.

The Crowes were keen to make Kiplin their home, as well as put their mark indelibly on the house. They commenced a programme of alterations, which included a central staircase, fashionable ceiling mouldings, dado rails and fireplaces.

In 1817 the great-great-granddaughter of Christopher Crowe, Sarah Crowe, married John Delaval Carpenter, 4th Earl of Tyrconnel. A year later she inherited Kiplin. Many believe that the crest which can be found above the front entrance is that of the Calvert family, but it actually belongs to the Carpenters and the motto 'per acuta belli', meaning 'by the stratagems of war', is thought to be a reference to their naval background.

Unfortunately, the couple only had one daughter, who died in infancy, and as there were no children to inherit the estate it was passed on to a cousin, Admiral Walter Talbot. A condition of the will, however, was that he should change his name to Carpenter.

In 1938 Miss Bridget Talbot was made joint owner of Kiplin by her cousin Sarah Carpenter, who had inherited the estate in 1904. Bridget was an astounding lady, who had not only been a great traveller, but was also a passionate political activist and reformer. She was awarded the Italian Medal for Valour for her work on the Italian–Austrian front with the Red Cross during World War One. She also invented a waterproof torch for lifebelts, and then proceeded to campaign tirelessly for their compulsory provision to all Royal Navy,

St Mary's Church at Bolton on Swale, near Kiplin Hall.

Merchant Navy and RAF personnel. By using both her social and political connections she successfully made this a reality and in doing so saved countless lives.

During World War Two the hall was requisitioned by the military. It was initially used by the army but in 1942 it was taken over by the RAF. Sadly, the house suffered much damage from its military occupation and for years after the war Bridget tried in vain to obtain compensation. Establishing a charitable trust in 1968, she declared that it was her wish to preserve Kiplin Hall for the benefit of the nation. This magnificent Jacobean country house lies halfway between Richmond and Northallerton and is open to the public.

RICHMOND

Richmond is an attractive market town on the River Swale. It is unusual among the other towns and villages in the Yorkshire Dales as most derive their names from either Old Norse or Anglo-Saxon words, whereas Richmond comes from Old French and means a strong hill.

In 1258 a Franciscan friary was built on land which had been donated by Ralph Fitz Randal, Lord of Middleham. Originally, the church had been made from timber but it was later replaced by a more permanent stone structure. A document which was written in 1386 tells us that the friary consisted of the church, a dormitory, a refectory, a parlour, a warden's house, a room for teaching called 'the studies', a washroom and a guesthouse.

In January 1539 it was dissolved and, after a period of ownership by the Crown, it passed into private hands. Many of the original buildings have long vanished; however, the warden's house survived and for a number of years it was used by Richmond Grammar School as the headmaster's house. It has since become part of the hospital.

Before defeating Richard III at Bosworth in 1485 Henry VII was Earl of Richmond. In 1502 he renamed the hamlet of Sheen (now in Greater London) after his earldom in Yorkshire when he built his new palace there. A previous Earl of Richmond was Arthur, Constable de Richemont (1393–1458), who fought alongside

*The remains of
Richmond Friary.*

Joan of Arc against the English. This Frenchman had been granted his English title while still a child.

The town possesses one of the oldest English theatres still in use: the Theatre Royal, which was opened in 1788 by Samuel Butler (1750–1812). In 1830 it was closed and for over 100 years it was used for a number of other purposes, including as a furniture warehouse. In the early 1960s it was restored to its former glory and it was reopened as a theatre in May 1963 by the Princess Royal. Remarkably, many of the theatre's early features were found to still be intact.

During the Middle Ages this delightful market town had been Swaledale's centre for the woollen industry, but its prosperity would increase further during the late 17th and 18th centuries as the demand for its goods increased as a result of the expanding lead mining industry in nearby Arkengarth. This growth in wealth meant that the town was virtually rebuilt in the 18th century and many of its buildings

are still unmistakably Georgian. It has been variously referred to as the 'Heart of the Dales' or the 'Gateway to Swaledale', and is unquestionably one of the most romantic towns in North Yorkshire.

RICHMOND CASTLE

The impressive Richmond Castle was constructed shortly after the Norman Conquest as a result of the English uprising in York in 1069 in which the garrison was slaughtered. It is one of the oldest stone castles in the country and is located high above the River Swale. Built on a rocky promontory in the shape of a triangle with two sides being steep cliffs (known as Riche Mount), it was an ideal location for defence. The castle also holds the distinction of containing the oldest great hall in England, called Scolland's Hall, which was named after the castle's first constable, who died in 1150 after 60 years of loyal service. The hall consisted of two storeys that included the great hall and a solar, which was the lord's private chamber:

The magnificent Richmond Castle dominates the town of Richmond and can be seen for many miles around.

these would normally be located on the first floor behind the high table and were accessible from the great hall. Often they would be built in the protected side of the keep to allow the inclusion of windows instead of the usual slits, thus allowing for maximum sunlight.

The original keep was located at the gatehouse; however, a new one was constructed in the 12th century which was 100 foot high and had walls that were 11 foot thick. This work was commenced by Duke Conan the Little and was completed by Henry II, who strengthened the castle's defences by adding walls, towers and a barbican. The castle was mentioned in the *Domesday Book* as the 'castlery of Richmond'. Normally, castles of this period were made of wood, but Richmond Castle was from the very beginning constructed from stone. This, combined with the fact that throughout its history it was to see very little military action, means that it remains one of the country's best-preserved Norman castles.

The castle's first owner was Alain Le Roux de Ponthievre of Brittany (Alan the Red). He was nephew to William the Conqueror and was granted the lands in 1071. It remained in family hands for another 100 years until the death of Duke Conan (great-nephew to Alan the Red) when Henry II took over the Honour of Richmond. While still alive, Conan had become a potential threat to the throne as he had become too wealthy and in 1166 Henry II persuaded him to relinquish Brittany to the king, as well as betrothing his only daughter Constance to Henry's eldest son Geoffrey.

According to legend, King Arthur lies sleeping in a cavern beneath Richmond Castle. There he waits until England faces grave peril and, along with his knights, he will rise to defend this green and pleasant land. It is said that under this remarkable castle lie a number of secret tunnels and a story tells of a potter named Thompson who explored one of these tunnels. As he delved into its depths he discovered King Arthur and his knights all asleep and nearby he found a sword and a horn. Thompson took the horn and, just as he was about to put it to his lips the knights began to wake. As he fled in terror, he heard a voice call from behind:

Potter Thompson, Potter Thompson,

If thou hadst drawn the sword or blown the horn,

Thou hadst been the luckiest man e'er born.

But this is the stuff of legends.

THE GREEN HOWARDS

In the main square of Richmond stands the Green Howards Regimental Museum. The collection was started shortly after World War One, when many items were brought back from the trenches. At first the collection, which mainly consisted of medals and badges, was kept at the barracks. But it had no permanent home and led a nomadic existence, being moved from room to room. In 1955 the growing collection was moved out of the barracks and into a wooden hut that had once been used by the 4th Battalion (TA). The museum was now open to the public, but they would have had the doubtful pleasure of passing under the watchful eyes of a drill sergeant to reach the hut and view the martial relics. When the barracks closed in 1961, the museum was again moved, this time to the stone gymnasium. Much work was required

This is the crest of the Green Howards which can be seen above the entrance to the regimental museum. It was designed by the regiment's patron Princess Alexandria of Denmark, Queen Consort to Edward VII. The letter 'A' can clearly be seen incorporated in the design.

to convert this old barn-like building into an acceptable venue for the collection, but it was through the hard work and determination of a small band of men, most notably Colonel Jonathan Forbes, Brigadier Tommy Collins and John Goat, who was the first attendant of the museum, that the building was to become a fine regimental museum. However, it soon became apparent that the building was not ideal as the Home Office, who had taken over the other buildings, had converted these into an approved school. Security had become a major problem and it was evident that they would have to find somewhere else to house the museum and quickly.

It was through one of those moments of serendipity that the solution to their problem was found. Colonel Forbes was entertaining a fellow former officer, Major Peter Kirby, at the King's Head in the centre of Richmond. The Major had been an officer in the 4th Green Howards during World War Two, but was now the curator of the Royal Welsh Fusiliers Museum. During the meal the Colonel explained their predicament and the Major, pointing through the window to the disused Holy Trinity Church which stood opposite, remarked that the building was ideal for their museum.

The Diocese of Ripon was prepared to let the church for a peppercorn rent, but the cost of reconstruction would be astronomical. It would take the regiment and its supporters two years to collect the £90,000 needed to carry out the work on this mediaeval church. The main body of the old church was converted into the museum, but a large stained-glass window and a small chapel, where 24 people could worship, were kept. In July 1973 the museum was officially opened by King Olaf V of Norway, the Colonel-in-Chief of the Green Howards, and in the first year it attracted over 36,000 visitors. Although the museum was to be runner-up in the Museum of the Year Awards in 1975, attendance figures would soon begin to dwindle. The museum had

been designed by regimental officers for other officers and soldiers, and so failed to attract the general visitors, who were drawn to the other attractions in the area, which were thrilling their visitors with modern displays and making full use of current technologies. Something had to be done if the museum was to survive and this important collection was to continue. So, in May 1995 the trustees of the museum gave the 'green light' on a set of plans that would rejuvenate the flagging attendance. Later that year refurbishment was to begin, which, although it would take only four months to complete, would add many exciting improvements to the museum, such as audio-visual systems and touch screens. The modernisation had the desired effect and soon the museum was drawing back the crowds and yet again winning awards. Once more the future began to look rosy and in 1998 it was awarded the coveted Yorkshire Tourist's Boards White Rose Award.

Since then things have not stood still and in 2006 the museum successfully applied for a grant from the Heritage Lottery Fund, which meant that work could begin on the ground-floor gallery. Included in these new alterations was a new entrance with a museum shop next to it and a kids' zone, with a number of exciting activities to entertain children.

Although the regiment was first formed in 1688 by Colonel Francis Luttrell, it was not until 1744 during the Wars of the Austrian Succession that the regiment became known as the 'Green Howards'. The convention of the time was for a regiment to be known by the name of its colonel and during the campaign the regimental Colonel was the Honourable Charles Howard. At that time it was brigaded with another regiment, whose colonel also had the surname of Howard. This caused some confusion and it was necessary to have some of form of distinction between the two regiments. Charles Howard's regiment wore green facings on their uniforms, whereas the other regiment wore theirs with buff facings. It therefore seemed logical for them to be called the 'Green Howards' and the others the 'Buff Howards'. This nickname stuck until it became the official name of the regiment in 1920.

In 1782 the regiment began its long association with the North Riding of Yorkshire, when it became known as 'The 19th (First Yorkshire North Riding Regiment) of Foot'. However, it was not until almost 100 years later that they were actually based in Yorkshire. In 1873 the regiment made its home in the North Yorkshire town of Richmond. Two years later, the regiment was presented with new colours by the then Princess of Wales (later Queen Alexandra), formerly a Princess of the Royal House of Denmark. The new colours were to replace those carried throughout the Crimean War and the regiment was granted the title of 'The Princess of Wales's Own'. A short time later the title was changed to 'The Princess of Wales's Own Yorkshire Regiment' when the territorial system was introduced, while in 1920 the regimental title finally became 'The Green Howards (Alexandra, Princess of Wales's Own Yorkshire)'. It is interesting to note the regimental cap badge was designed by the Princess and incorporates the Cross of Denmark (the Dannebrog) and her initial, with a Princess's coronet above it. The date on the badge denotes the year that the regiment became the Princess's own and the roman numerals represent the 19th Regiment of Foot.

The regiment has had an illustrious history since it first saw action at the Battle of the Boyne in Ireland in 1690. It was to receive its first battle honour fighting with the Duke of Marlborough at Malplaquet. Since then the regiment has taken part in every major campaign involving the British army. Its roll of honour is long and impressive and includes: Belle Isle, the American War of Independence, the Siege of Ostend, Alma, Inkerman, Sevastopol, Relief of Kimberley, Paardeberg,

South Africa 1899–1902; World War One – Ypres 1914, 1915, 1917, Langemarck 1914, 1917, Gheluvelt, Neuve Chapelle, St Julien, Frezenburg, Bellewaarde, Aubers, Festubert 1915, Loos, Somme 1916–1918, Albert 1916, Bazentin, Poziers, Flers-Courcelet, Morval, Thiepval, Le Transloy, Ancre Heights, Ancre 1916, Arras 1917, 1918, Scarpe 1917–18, Messines 1917, 1918 Pilckem, Menin Road, Polygon Wood, Broodseinde, Poelcappelle, Passchendaele, Cambrai 1917–18, St Quentin, Hindenburg Line, Canal du Nord, Beaurevoir, Selle Valenciennes, Sambre, France and Flanders 1914–18, Piave Vittorio Veneto, Italy 1917–18, Suvla, Landing at Suvla, Scimitar Hill, Gallipoli 1915, Egypt 1916, Archangel 1918, Afghanistan 1919; World War Two – Otta, Norway 1940, Defence of Arras, Dunkirk 1940, Normandy Landing, Tilly sur Seulles, St Pierre La Vielle, Gheel Nede'rijn, North West Europe 1940, 1944–45, Gazala, Defence of Alamein Line, El Alamein, Mareth, Akarit, North Africa 1942–43, Landing in Sicily, Lentini, Sicily 1943, Minturno, Anzio, Italy 1943–44, Arakan Beaches and Burma 1945.

The Battle of Alma has a particular significance to the regiment for it was not until after this battle that it received its Battle Honours for Malplaquet and Belle Isle, and consequently on 20 September each year the anniversary of Alma is celebrated. The regiment is still distinguishing itself to this day and added to their honours as a mark of recognition the following Yorkshire towns of Beverley, Bridlington, Middlesbrough, Northallerton, Pickering, Redcar, Richmond and Scarborough, who have all granted the regiment the status of honorary freeman.

ASKE HALL AND THE MARQUIS OF ZETLAND

Travel only one and a half miles north of Richmond and you will come to Aske Hall. The land was purchased by Sir Conyers D'Arcy in

The magnificent Aske Hall.

1727 from the Aske family. When Sir Conyers originally purchased the estate it had consisted of a pele tower dating from the 12th century, some surviving sections of a 15th-century hall and a lofty two-storey manorial hall built in 1578. These were surrounded by bare and swampy fields. The estate had been allowed to fall into a state of disrepair; but by 1727 he had commenced a number of improvements to the property.

However, it was Sir Lawrence Dundas, who purchased the property in 1763, who was to create one of the finest country seats in the region. He employed the famous architect, John Carr, to transform the property into a 'suitable seat for a new dynasty'. Sir Lawrence was an extremely ambitious and successful man, who was aware that the Aske estate included the pocket borough of Richmond and that by purchasing the property he would be able to nominate the MP.

Although he was a successful and influential man, whose business interests included banking and property, despite his best efforts he was never to achieve his greatest wish: obtaining a peerage. This honour would go to his son Thomas Dundas (1741–1820), who in 1794 was created Baron Dundas of Aske. His grandson, also called Lawrence (1766–1839), was created 1st Earl of Zetland in 1838. When the 2nd Earl, Thomas Dundas (1795–1873) died without children, the title and estate passed to his nephew Lawrence Dundas (1844–1929), who became 3rd Earl of Zetland and subsequently the 1st Marquis of Zetland.

To this day, Aske Hall and the title of Marquis of Zetland are still held by the Dundas family. It is open to the public on a very limited number of days per year and for guided tours only.

EASBY ABBEY

The ruins of the 12th-century Abbey of St Agatha, which stand at Easby, were founded in 1152 by Roald, the Constable of Richmond. The abbey was run by Premonstratensians, also known as Norbertines, which was a Catholic religious order of canons, rather than monks. Their attire of white habits led to them being known as the white canons. Unlike other orders, they were exempt from the strict episcopal discipline; however, they followed an austere code which was similar to that of the Cistercian monks.

Like many of the religious buildings in the north of England, Easby suffered during the frequent Scottish raids of the Middle Ages. The greatest damage, however, would ironically be caused by the English army while billeting here en route to the Battle of Neville's Cross, which took place on 17 October 1346. The Scots had crossed the border into England on 7 October in the erroneous belief that it would be completely unprotected, as Edward III was engaged in a major campaign in France. It would prove a costly error, as the English quickly mobilised an army in Richmond under William Zouche, the Archbishop of York.

Although it was not a very large contingent and would be outnumbered by about two to one, it took the Scots completely unawares and won a resounding victory with losses of about 200 men, while the Scottish army suffered casualties of over 7,000.

As with all other religious institutions, Easby was finally closed during the Dissolution and was left to fall into a state of ruin. Today the stunning ruins are cared for by English Heritage, and a number of its fine features have been saved for posterity.

MUKER

The earliest known human occupation of the land around the village of Muker dates back to the Bronze Age. In the early years of the 20th century a skeleton with a number of flint tools was unearthed and it is believed that this may have been a Bronze Age burial site. The village is located at the tributary of the River Swale and the Straw Beck which, combined with the

These are the ruins of the 12th-century Abbey of St Agatha at Easby.

The Literary Institute at Muker was built in 1867. It cost £260 to construct, of which nearly half was given by William Tarn and the rest raised by subscription. It contained over 600 books.

The Church of St Mary in Muker was one of the few churches to be constructed during the reign of Elizabeth I. It was consecrated on 3 August 1580 by William Chatterton, the Bishop of Chester.

abundance of lush meadowland, meant that Muker was an ideal location. The Vikings were quick to recognise its advantages and in settling there they were able to make a good living from both agricultural and pastoral farming. The name Muker is thought to derive from the Old Norse 'Mjoraker', meaning narrow acre.

Until the late 18th century the economy of the village was based solely on farming; however, Muker was soon to take advantage of the increased importance of the lead mining industry, which was flourishing in the region. It had also become a major centre for hand-knitting. When the mining industry declined at the end of the 19th century the village resorted to farming for its livelihood.

In 1580 the church of St Mary the Virgin was constructed on the site where a chapel of ease had once stood. With the consecration of the church and graveyard the population of Upper Swaledale were no longer forced to undertake

the arduous journey to the parish church in Grinton to bury their dead. In 1891 the church was restored; however, the tower, nave and chancel are all original and date from the reign of Elizabeth I.

The village is the home of the famous brass band called the Muker Silver Band, which was formed in 1897. Although Muker has only a tiny population the band is still going strong and is now one of the last remaining in the region. The locals are fiercely loyal to it, and it has members aged from 10 to 70. With a busy calendar of public performances, it has a wide repertoire ranging from ancient classics to more modern pieces.

THE WILDLIFE PHOTOGRAPHER FROM THWAITE

Born in 1871 in the small Swaledale village of Thwaite, Cherry Kearton was to grow up to become one of the world's earliest wildlife photographers and a great pioneer. From humble origins he would one day become the friend of the American President, Theodore Roosevelt, whom he was to film in a documentary called *Roosevelt in Africa*, which he made in 1910. Cherry was also the childhood hero of and a great inspiration to the naturalist Sir David Attenborough.

Cherry's interest in nature, like many boys who grew up in the countryside, developed at an early age. Both he and his brother, Richard, would rise at four in the morning to roam the country lanes and further their nature studies. It was while climbing a tree one day in search of birds' nests that Richard fell and broke his leg. Unfortunately, the injury was poorly set by a doctor and he was lame for the rest of his life. Unable to play the usual games with the other village boys, his grandfather taught him to love birds. It was his love of nature which eventually led to him becoming a writer.

In the autumn of 1882 Richard was offered a job at the publishing house of Cassell's by Sidney

Galpin, who was the son of one of the company's founders. Richard left for London and on 10 October 1882 he began what would become a very successful career in writing, broadcasting, publishing and lecturing. In 1887, on the death of their father John Kearton, Cherry left Swaledale to join his brother in London and began a famous collaboration with his brother, which resulted in the publication of a number of books. The first book was published in 1885 and was called *British Birds' Nests and Egg Collecting* (a pastime which is now illegal). Richard wrote the text and Cherry illustrated the book with his experimental photographs, which had been taken on a cheap second-hand camera. Many more books were to follow.

Cherry was a keen experimenter in the art of wildlife photography, and armed with his camera and a good head for heights he fearlessly scaled the sea cliffs of the remote Scottish islands in search of images. His photographs of St Kilda, which were taken shortly before the island was permanently evacuated, have now become extremely important documents and record an almost forgotten past. In 1894 Cherry left Cassell's to pursue a career in the freelance filming and photography of wildlife.

This is the carved lintel above the front door to Cherry and Richard Kearton's childhood home.

During World War One Cherry served with the 25th Battalion of the Royal Fusiliers in East Africa. His previous experience and first-hand knowledge of Africa made Captain Kearton an ideal choice for Intelligence Officer. After the war he married his second wife Ada Forrest, who had been a famous opera singer, but she gave up this successful career to accompany and support Cherry on his many filming trips. On 27 September 1940, as he left Broadcasting House after making a children's programme about wildlife, he collapsed in the street and died. A memorial plaque to Cherry is located at his old school in Muker.

WENSLEY

The settlement of Wensley was once the most important market town in the whole of Wensleydale: so important that it gave its name to the dale. This makes Wensleydale unusual as most of the other dales are named after rivers. In 1563 the town suffered from a catastrophe from which it would never recover. The Great Plague struck and many perished. Those who escaped this scourge simply fled to neighbouring Leyburn, which they considered a much healthier place, and with the influx of these terrified people the settlement at Leyburn began to grow and prosper.

Wensley is an ancient settlement which dates back to at least Anglo-Saxon times and its name

This is the memorial to Cherry Kearton on the front wall of the former village school at Muker.

The village of Wensley.

Opposite: Built in 1698, Ivelet Bridge was constructed to take an old packhorse trail across the River Swale. This trail also runs parallel to a more ancient 'corpse way', along which the bodies of the dead were taken from the villages and hamlets to St Andrew's at Grinton for burial.

The reliquary, which is thought to contain the remains of St Agatha, at Holy Trinity in Wensley.

means 'Wændel's clearing'. In the 11th century written documents record it as Wendreslaga. In 1202 King John allowed a market to be held in the village after being given a horse by Hugh Malebiche. Over 100 years later James de Wensley obtained the right to hold a market on

each Wednesday, as well as an annual fair. These would have brought much prosperity to the town; however, both the markets and the annual fair have long been abandoned. All that remains of the village's mediaeval splendour are the fine church and the 15th-century stone bridge. It is thought that the bridge was built with £40, which had been left in a will by the first Lord Scrope, which he had bequeathed to repair the earlier bridge.

Holy Trinity in Wensley is a delightful 13th-century church, which was built on the foundation of an earlier Saxon church. Built into the interior walls are a number of interesting carved Saxon stones, while inside the church can be found a number of furnishings which were rescued from Easby Abbey at the time of the Dissolution of the Monasteries. These include choir pews, a reliquary and a screen, which was used to form the Scrope family pew. The reliquary, which is Gothic in design, is of particular interest as it is believed to contain the remains of St Agatha, and is thought to be to be the only wooden one left in England. It is unusual in that it also has a poor

Far right: This is one of a number of interesting Anglo-Saxon carvings which can be found in Holy Trinity in Wensley.

Far right: This is a wonderful example of a Jacobean font in Holy Trinity on which some of the letters have been engraved upside down.

The evening light shining on the 'Shawl' in Leyburn.

box attached to its front. The church has a fine example of a Jacobean font which is inscribed and some of the letters have been carved upside down.

In 1678 Lord Bolton moved out of Bolton Castle and built his new home at Wensley. However, there seems to be some debate as to when the actual construction of Bolton Hall began as, although the rainwater heads are dated 1678, some argue that it was actually built in 1655. But the later date seems more probable and Nicholas Pevsner notes that the earlier date does not fit with the building's architectural style. The hall was totally burnt out in 1902 and now only the shell remains.

LEYBURN

The name Leyburn is thought to mean 'shelter by the stream' from the Anglo-Saxon words *hleg* (shelter) and *burna* (stream). Before the 16th century it had been little more than a sleepy hamlet, high on the bank of the River Ure. Its fortunes were to change dramatically after the plague had struck Wensley. As already noted above, it was considered much healthier than its

neighbour and with the sudden influx of people Leyburn's population grew rapidly. In 1684 it was granted a charter which entitled the town to hold markets and a fair and this further increased its prosperity. By the 1800s the population had doubled.

The town's main feature is the 'Shawl', which is a natural limestone terrace that overlooks Leyburn. It is thought to have been given its name when Mary, Queen of Scots, accidently dropped her shawl there while fleeing from captivity from the nearby Bolton Castle. The shawl was discovered by her pursuers and her whereabouts were then betrayed. It is said that a young guard had aided her in her escape. Sadly, there is no truth in this romantic story, and the name is actually derived from the Viking word *Skali* meaning 'huts', as it would once have had shelters for shepherds located there.

ASKRIGG

In the Middle Ages Upper Wensleydale was covered by the Wensley Forest and was the hunting grounds of the lords of Middleham. The settlement of Askrigg lay just outside the

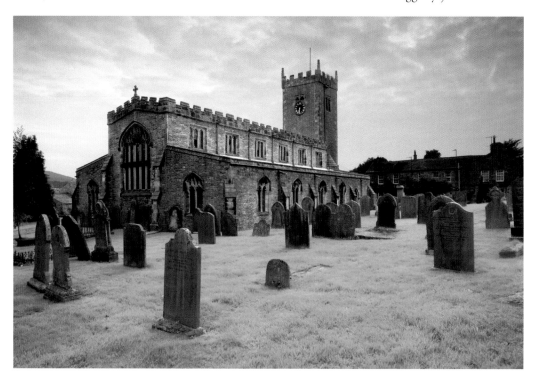

The magnificent church of St Oswald in Askrigg was constructed in the Perpendicular style in 1466.

forest and therefore was free from the strict forest laws. The name Askrigg is derived from Old Norse *Askr Hryggr* meaning 'Ash Ridge'. The settlement was to develop into an important trading place and in 1587 it was granted a royal charter by Elizabeth I. This enabled the town to hold regular markets and to collect fees from the traders, thereby bringing in much wealth to the community.

Each year, according to the charter, four men were to be elected from the inhabitants of the town. These men were to be responsible for the collecting of the tolls and the custody of the toll booth, which was located close to the market cross. The toll booth was a two-storey building, in which the lower floor had once been used as a lock-up or 'dungeon' in the days of the old parish constables. In 1880 the holders of this office were W.E.M. Winn, Richard Mason, Robert Mason and Metcalfe Graham.

Traditionally, textiles and wool were the main goods traded at the town, and Askrigg would also become renowned for hand-knitting. The town also gained a reputation for clock-making, when in 1680 a Quaker named John Ogden moved there. He was to make clocks in Askrigg for the next 40 years and the industry was to continue well into the 19th century.

At the foot of the market cross can be found the 'Bull Ring'. Originally, this would have been used to tie up a bull, which would be baited by dogs. Fortunately, this barbaric practice has now long been abolished. The ring also had another use, for it appears a custom grew up in the town whereby a man wishing to fight would

An old stone font in St Oswald's.

*Mill Gill Foss:
Even as late as the
20th century
almost every
village would have
had its own small
quarry where stone
could be obtained
for building work.
Most accessible
rock outcrops
would have been
used, especially
exposed areas at
waterfalls such as
Mill Gill Foss, near
Askrigg.*

Great and Small, which was based on a collection of books by Alf Wight, about a fictitious Yorkshire vet named James Herriot. Those who remember the series may recognise the King's Arms as being the Drovers' Arms and Cringley House as the vets' surgery called 'Skeldale House'.

NAPPA HALL

Built in 1459 by James Metcalfe, Nappa Hall is one of North Yorkshire's few remaining castellated homes. It was constructed at a time when its inhabitants would have been living in fear of the frequent raids from over the border. The land was granted to the Metcalfes for their services at Agincourt when they followed the Scropes of Bolton Castle. A small tenement stood on the land, which was mockingly called 'No Castle'; however, James was a deeply proud man of ambition and soon applied for and was granted permission to build a battlemented hall. Over the centuries, the family continued to prosper and during the reign of Henry VI a Metcalfe became Chancellor of the Duchy of Lancaster. The Metcalfes were also loyal

turn the bull ring over, and if another felt similarly inclined he would turn it back and a fight would ensue.

A number of the buildings in Askrigg were used for the popular TV series *All Creatures*

Nappa Hall.

Nappa Hall with Nappa Scar in the distance.

supporters of Henry VIII and fought at Flodden Field when the Scots attempted to invade England en masse under the banner of James IV of Scotland, in an attempt to divert the English troops away from their campaign against the French.

It was during the Tudor period that the Metcalfe family fortunes were at their height and life at Nappa Hall would have been exciting, with lavish entertainment, feasting and merriment. Nappa Hall was to entertain many important guests: once a hunting party turned up which included Mary, Queen of Scots, among them. But this high living was not to last forever, and soon the fortunes of the Metcalfe family fell into decline. It had been the Scropes who had given the first James Metcalfe the land, but generations later, through malice and envy, a Scrope requested his lawyers find out what legal claim the Metcalfes had on the land and property. It transpired that they had no claim whatsoever. Therefore, to remain at Nappa Hall, the occupying Metcalfe, Sir Christopher, was forced to sell and mortgage his estates. This, combined with his high living, resulted in the

severe depletion of the family fortunes. A century later the Metcalfes would lose the hall as the financial disaster of the South Sea Bubble wiped out the last of their money.

Nappa Hall became a farmhouse and while the kitchen remained a hive of activity, the high hall grew quiet, except on rainy days when it became a refuge for the children. Over time the hall became deserted and derelict. However, it was purchased in September 2008 by Mr D. Mark Thompson, who intends to restore it as his private residence. The public may view this fine historic building by appointment (and for a small donation).

BAINBRIDGE AND THE SHORTEST RIVER IN ENGLAND

From 'Bridge on the River Bain', the name of the village is derived from Old Norse and means 'short one'. This is an apt name, for the River Bain is said to be the shortest river in England at just two and a half miles long. The river is fed from Semerwater, which is the largest natural lake in North Yorkshire.

Semerwater.

According to legend, a proud town once stood at Semerwater and now lies beneath its waters. One night a poor old man arrived in the town. Tired and hungry from his long journey, he went from house to house in search of food and shelter. But at each dwelling he received the same uncharitable response and was turned away into the night. The last house he came to belonged to a lonely shepherd and his wife, so poor were they that they could hardly make ends meet. When they saw the poor old man, however, they were immediately filled with pity and took him in. They fed him and gave him shelter for the night.

The Carlow Stone is said to have been hurled at the Devil by a giant.

The River Bain is thought to be the shortest river in England and is just two and a half miles long. It flows from Semerwater and joins the River Ure at Bainbridge.

A weir at Bainbridge.

The next day the old man left the town and, turning, he raised his arms and spoke a dreadful curse: 'Semerwater rise! Semerwater sink! And swallow the town, all save this house, where they gave me meat and drink.' As soon as the words had left his mouth the waters of Semerwater gurgled up and drowned the occupants of this uncharitable town...all except the shepherd and his wife. Evidence of a Bronze Age village has been found in the lake, so perhaps this legend is more than a fanciful tale.

The attractive village of Bainbridge maintains an ancient custom: from 14 September to Shrove Tuesday a horn is blown at 9pm each night to help guide travellers who are crossing the fells. For many years the custom was kept by the Metcalfe family. The horn is kept behind the bar at the Rose and Crown. The original horn was made from cow's horn (and is also displayed behind the bar) but in 1864 a new horn of African ox was presented to the village.

In 1712 Dr Fothergill, the founder of the Quaker school at Ackworth (see *Exploring West Yorkshire's History*), was born at Carr End, near Bainbridge. The village was also the site of a Roman fort, which was called Virosidum. Nearby there are also the remains of a Roman road.

AYSGARTH FALLS

Aysgarth Falls have been attracting visitors for over 200 years, including such famous names as Ruskin, Turner and Wordsworth. William Wordsworth came here on his honeymoon with his new bride Mary Hutchinson.

The name Aysgarth originates from Old Norse and means 'an open space among the oak trees'. The falls are made up of a triple flight of waterfalls, which, when the River Ure is in full

The bridge at Bainbridge.

The thundering waters at Aysgarth Falls.

thunder, roar at an alarming rate. In 2005 they featured in the television series *Seven Natural Wonders*, which was broadcast on BBC2.

Aysgarth Falls.

YORE BRIDGE

In 1784 the Birkbeck family of Settle built Yore Mill to produce calico and other cotton goods. They located their mill below the upper Aysgarth Falls to take full advantage of its fast flowing waters, which were needed to power the mill's machinery. Spanning the river next to the mill stands Yore Bridge, which was designed by John Carr in 1793. This replaced an earlier packhorse bridge that had originally been built in 1539.

Yore Mill, which is now a Grade II listed building, has the distinction of once supplying the red flannel which was used to make the shirts worn by Garibaldi's army. In 1852 the mill was destroyed by fire, but was rebuilt the following year and the new structure was twice the size of the old building. The upper storeys of the new mill were used for the carding and spinning of knitting yarns, while the lower storey was used for the grinding of corn. In 1912 the whole mill was converted into a flour-rolling plant, and operated until 1958 when the production of flour ceased. It was then used to store cattle feed until 1969.

Yore Mill and Yore Bridge at Aysgarth.

CARPERBY

Visiting the quaint village of Carperby it is hard to believe that it was once a promising market town. It was granted its charter in 1305, but sadly it never prospered and was overshadowed by its neighbours such as Askrigg, Hawes and Leyburn. It would later take advantage of the

Far Left:
Top: St Stephen's at Aysgarth.

Middle: This stunning rood screen, which is in St Stephen's, was saved from Jervaulx Abbey.

Bottom: Middleham Castle, founded by Robert FitzRalph in the 11th century, passed into the hands of the powerful Neville family in the 13th century. It was the home of Richard III when he was the Lord of the North and became one of the strongest castles in the North of England.

Left: The market cross at Caperby.

lead mining industry in the region and would enjoy a modicum of prosperity for a while; however, it remained essentially an agricultural village.

A remarkable feature of the village is its market cross, which has faces carved on the sides. This impressive structure was erected in 1674 and it is believed that it was constructed to replace an earlier one. It was at Carperby that Alf Wight, the author of the James Herriot series of books, spent his honeymoon.

BOLTON CASTLE

In 1379 the 12-year-old Richard II granted Sir Richard le Scrope permission to convert his manor house into a feudal fortress. It would take 20 years and £12,000 (which at the time was an enormous amount of money) to complete Bolton Castle. The castle had many amazing improvements and some of the latest technological advances of its day. Even over 100

years later the castle created a stir for John Leland, who had been appointed the King's Antiquarian by Henry VIII and enthusiastically wrote about this stupendous stronghold's futuristic features, such as the chimneys which had been built into the walls to remove the smoke: a far cry from the crude hole in the roof. Others, it appears, were not so impressed by this, for they felt that the smoke hardened the timbers and was also beneficial to the health of the occupants.

Perhaps it is for the imprisonment of Mary, Queen of Scots, that the castle is most famous. In April 1568 she had fled to England following her defeat at the Battle of Langside. She had made her way to Carlisle, and it was probably here that she had wished to remain; however, the English had other ideas. Carlisle was too close to the Scottish border and consequently proved too dangerous. It was imperative that she was moved to a safe

The stupendous Bolton Castle.

distance, and for this Bolton Castle was considered ideal.

At the time Lord Scrope was at court, but he immediately set off north in the company of Sir Francis Knollys, with the aim of taking charge of Mary. It would be necessary to proceed with care and extreme diplomacy, for officially Mary was not a prisoner. When the subject of moving her was eventually mentioned, she quickly asked whether it would be of her own free will or as a captive. She was tactfully informed that it was the dear wish of Elizabeth I that she be moved closer to herself. This appeared to pacify her for the time being, but when the day came for her to move to Bolton Castle she proved not to be so composed and began to weep and rage in temper. Eventually, however, her tantrums abated when she realised that they were not having any effect, and she resigned herself to the inevitable.

On 16 July 1568 she arrived at Bolton Castle with only the clothes which she was standing in, and Lord Scrope was forced to write to James Stuart, Earl of Moray, at Loch Leven Castle, asking for her belongings to be forwarded to Bolton Castle. She remained at Bolton until 26 January 1569 when she was moved to Tutbury Castle in Staffordshire.

During the English Civil War the Parliamentarians laid siege to Bolton Castle. The Royalist garrison inside held out for six months, but without supplies (they had even eaten their last horse) the stronghold eventually fell and on 5 November 1645 they surrendered to the Parliamentarian forces, which were led by Major General Poyntz. The garrison troops were allowed to leave with their flags flying, but as a final act of defiance their commander Colonel Henry Chaytor cut off his own hand and flung it from the battlements at the Parliamentarians below.

After the death of John Scrope from the plague in 1646, the castle was left to his sister Mary. She married Charles Paulet, who would

An old railway sign.

become the 1st Duke of Bolton. In 1675 he built Bolton Hall in the village of Wensley as their new home. In 1794, with no male heirs to inherit the estate and title, the property passed to Jean Mary Paulet. After marrying Thomas Orde, who was a politician and Governor of Ireland, he added the Paulet name to his, but changed it to Orde-Powlett. Today the castle is owned by the 8th Lord of Bolton.

HAWES

On the River Ure in Upper Wensleydale stands the small market town of Hawes. Its name is derived from Anglo-Saxon and means a 'pass between hills'. This settlement has long been a popular destination for walkers and it is an excellent base from which to explore the magnificent countryside of this outstanding dale. Not only was this town once a centre for the lead mining industry, but it was also known for rope-making and the production of the world-famous Wensleydale cheese. Although lead mining has long since vanished from the area, the other two industries are still thriving in the town.

Wensleydale cheese was first made by monks in the Middle Ages using a recipe which had been brought to the region by French Cistercian monks when they settled in the area in 1150. The monks used ewes milk to produce this distinctive cheese. After the monasteries were

A carved wooden shepherd at Hawes…

…and his sheep!

closed in the 16th century the wives of local farmers took over its production and subsequently maintained its tradition.

In the 1930s the production of Wensleydale cheese almost completely ceased, and if it had not been for a local man named Kit Calvert it

An interesting engraved door lintel.

might have been lost forever. In 1935 he opened a new creamery at Hawes, but it was not always an easy venture, for after nearly 40 years of production there were plans to close the factory. Fortunately, a local campaign saved the cheese-making. It would have been unthinkable to have lost this wonderful delicacy, for what would true Yorkshire folk have eaten with their Christmas cake? And what would Wallace and Gromit have had for tea?

HARDRAW FORCE

Hardraw Force is the highest waterfall in England and has been attracting visitors for many centuries. Among its famous visitors are William Wordsworth, who visited the fall with his sister Dorothy in December 1799; the art critic and social thinker John Ruskin (1819–1900); and J.M.W. Turner (1775–1851), who painted it in about 1816.

The waterfall drops 100 feet from a rocky overhang, and it is possible to walk behind the column of water; however, although Wordsworth and numerous others have done so, the modern visitor is strongly discouraged from this. Due to it being a natural amphitheatre with excellent acoustics it became popular with the Victorians, who staged concerts and brass band competitions here. The tightrope walker Jean François Gravelet, better known as the great Blondin, who famously crossed the Niagara Falls in 1859, also crossed the chasm at Hardraw. It is said that he even stopped halfway along the rope and prepared an omelette.

To access the waterfall one must first go through the Green Dragon Inn. There is a small entrance fee, but the spectacle of this awesome waterfall is well worth the cost.

BEDALE

After the Norman Conquest Bedale was given to Bodin of Middleham by Count Alan le Roux (Alan the Red, 1040–1089), who had been a

The stunning Hardraw Force.

The market cross at Bedale.

Far right: The bridge over the River Ure at Middleham.

companion of William the Conqueror. Although the town was refounded after the 'Harrying of the North' by Scollandus, a Breton officer, there is no doubt that the origins of the settlement are much older. The name is derived from the Anglo-Saxon words 'Beda's halh', meaning a secret corner or retreat belonging to

Bede: there is no evidence to suggest that it was the Venerable Bede of Jarrow, which the name refers to, but conversely neither is there anything to suggest that it is not.

Many ancient artefacts can be found in Bedale's parish church of St Gregory, including a remarkable gravestone from the Viking period, which has the legend of Wayland, the mythical blacksmith, carved into it. It is said that if you leave your horse with a small silver coin at Wayland's Smithy (which is the name of a burial mound in Oxfordshire) it will be magically re-shod by the morning.

An interesting feature which stands on the banks of Bedale Beck is the Leech House. This unique 18th-century castellated building was

The Leech House at Bedale.

where the apothecary kept his stock of leeches, which were once commonly used in medical practice.

JERVAULX ABBEY

The Cistercian abbey of Jervaulx was founded in 1156 by John de Kinstan, who had been travelling with 12 other monks from Byland Abbey to visit another monastery at Fors. During their journey they became lost in thick woods, but were miraculously guided to safety by a vision of the Virgin Mary and Child, whichspoke to them saying 'Ye are late of Byland, but now of Yorevale'. The astonished monks took this to be a sign, and later returned to this site, where a new monastery was built for them by Conan, the 5th Earl of Richmond.

The name has been recorded in various forms: Jobevallis, Jorevalle, Yorevale (this is the Norse name for Wensleydale), Gervaux, Jervaux, Jervanix and Jervis, as well as the present Jervaulx. The abbey became renowned for the breeding of horses, and it was also here that Wensleydale cheese was first produced. At the height of its wealth the abbey owned half of the dale.

Jervaulx suffered greatly during the Dissolution of the Monasteries, and was reduced to a ruin through a savage campaign: this was due to Adam Sedbar, who was the last abbot, and his involvement in the Pilgrimage of Grace. Adam was taken to the Tower of London in 1537, and an inscription which he carved during his incarceration can still be seen on the wall of his cell. He was hanged at Tyburn in June 1537.

Henry VIII's destruction of the abbey was ruthless and complete; not only did all the valuables pass into the royal treasury, but also the roof of the church was stripped of its lead, which was a considerable amount and totalled in the region of 356 tons. The abbey's dressed stone became a valuable quarry for local building projects. When the first Earl of Ailesbury took ownership of this ruined abbey in the early 19th century he was faced with the daunting task of clearing away centuries of rubble and debris. After doing so he planted shrubs and evergreens in the grounds, and built a wall around the property to prevent further damage by vandals. Today these lovingly preserved ruins are open to the public.

MASHAM

The ancient market town of Masham is perhaps most famous for being the home of the award-winning Theakston Brewery. But apart from its brewing achievements, this town has many other features which deserve our investigation. Its market square is the largest in North Yorkshire and is surrounded by some delightful Georgian buildings. The square was also the site for an annual Sheep Fair, at which it is reputed as many as 80,000 sheep would have been sold in a good year. The sales would also have included animals from the flocks owned by the nearby abbeys of Fountains and Jervaulx. Although the annual fair is still held every September, it is now not on such a grand scale as those former days.

The town was to receive its first charter granting it the right to hold a market in 1250, which was followed by a further two charters in 1328 and 1393 respectively. Next to the

Masham's Town Hall: this building was used as a convalescent home for the Leeds Pals during World War One.

mediaeval market cross can be found a plaque to commemorate the granting of these charters.

Masham's early history is open to debate, but there is evidence of human activity going back to Neolithic times: at nearby Fearby there can be found a field called Standing Stones. On many of the surrounding hills there are lynchets (derived from the Anglo-Saxon word 'hlinc' meaning ridge), which are an early form of terracing created to aid cultivation, while beside the churchyard on Gregory Hill there are earthworks.

On 25 November 1350 the title of Baron Scrope of Masham was created. The first baron was Henry le Scrope, who was first cousin of Lord Richard le Scrope of Bolton Castle. The title was abolished 65 years later, when the third baron, also called Henry, was executed for high treason. He had been one of the principal

conspirators in the Southampton Plot of 1415. The plan had been to murder Henry IV as he was setting out for his invasion of France, but the plot was discovered and Scrope, along with his fellow schemers, was quickly arrested. After being dragged ignominiously through the streets of Southampton, he was put to death.

Henry was not, however, the only family member to plot against the king, for his uncle Richard le Scrope, who was the Archbishop of York, had joined with the Earl of Northumberland to rebel against Henry IV in 1404. The archbishop, who had previously enjoyed an amicable relationship with the king, found himself at odds with Henry after the taxation of Church lands had been proposed by the Unlearned Parliament. This parliament had been called by the king in 1404 with the sole purpose of raising money for his wars, which had placed a great drain on the royal coffers. It was also known as the Parliament of Dunces, the Lawless Parliament or the Parliamentum Indoctorum, for the king had refused to allow lawyers to stand as members.

There can be no doubt that the real mastermind behind the rebellion was the power-hungry Earl of Northumberland, who had manipulated the archbishop for his own ends. The earl had previously attempted an uprising, but had been forced to submit after his son had been killed during a fierce battle at Shrewsbury on 21 July 1403. It was while marching to his son's aid that he learned of his death. On this occasion the king showed clemency and pardoned the wayward earl, but in 1405 he would not be so lenient. The earl, however, evaded the king's wrath by escaping across the Scottish border, where he would remain for some years as a constant menace.

Scrope was not so fortunate, for he was captured and, along with another confederate, Thomas Mowbray, the Earl of Nottingham, was beheaded, despite appeals by the Archbishop of Canterbury, who had travelled to York, where their trial was being held, to beseech the king. The execution of Scrope created a profound shock throughout the land, which many would compare with the murder of Thomas Becket. In fact, such was the outrage that the king was almost excommunicated, and he undoubtedly would have been if it had not been for Pope Gregory XII's fear that, in doing so, Henry would have sided with the rival Pope in Avignon. Shortly afterwards, however, the king was struck down with a disfiguring illness which was rumoured by many to be leprosy and was attributed to the retribution of God. Scrope's body was buried in the north-east corner of York Minster and his tomb would become a place of pilgrimage for the people of the north.

The title of Baron Scrope of Masham was restored in 1426 with John Scrope becoming the 4th baron. After the death of the 11th baron, Geoffrey Scrope, in 1517 the title fell into abeyance and the estate was divided between his three sisters.

It is thought that the first church was built in the seventh century and stood on the site of the town hall. The present-day St Mary's, although possessing some Saxon stonework, is of Norman construction with later additions from the 15th century. In front of the main door can be found the large stump of a Saxon preaching cross. However, the years and the weather have not been kind to it and its once intricate carving has all but been worn away. Even so, it still affords an impressive sight. An interesting feature of the parish is that the vicar cannot be ordered to visit the archbishop, but must be invited. This originates from when Masham was given to the Minster of York in mediaeval times. The archbishop of the day, not wishing to travel so far north to oversee the town's affairs, granted the town a 'Peculier' court. This meant that the town had jurisdiction over its own affairs and gave its name to the world-famous

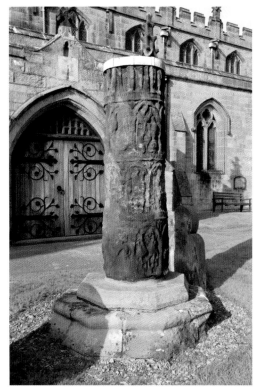

The remains of a Saxon preaching cross outside St Mary's in Masham.

This excellent example of an oriel window belongs to the Marmion Tower, which is a 15th-century gatehouse. The manor house to which it belongs has long since vanished. It was once the property of the Marmion family.

beer brewed by Theakston's: the deliciously dark *Old Peculier.*

Founded in 1827, Theakston's have been brewing beer for over 180 years. The brewery was originally founded by Robert Theakston at the Black Bull Inn. For a short period the brewery was owned by Scottish and Newcastle, but in 2003 it was bought back by the family. Masham is also the home of the Black Sheep Brewery, which was founded in 1992 by Paul Theakston as a result of the takeover of Theakston Brewery by Scottish and Newcastle in 1987.

The Leeds-born artist Julius Caesar Ibbetson (29 December 1759 – 13 October 1817) moved to Masham in 1804, where he was to spend the rest of his life. It is said that he was given his unusual middle name because he was delivered by caesarean section after his mother was killed in a tragic skating accident. While living in Masham he was to produce some of his finest paintings. He had been prompted to live in the town after meeting with the Yorkshire philanthropist William Danby and wishing to live near him. Julius was a kind man, who soon became popular with the townsfolk, and was to

The memorial for the four civilians and two soldiers who died when the Luftwaffe dropped two parachute mines on 16 April 1941.

play an active role in the community and the development of Masham. In 1803 he wrote and published his treatise on painting called *An Accidence, or Gamut, of Painting in Oil.* He is buried in the churchyard at St Mary's church in Masham, and inscribed on his gravestone are the words 'an artist eminent for his taste and skill in painting rustic figures, cattle and rural scenery'.

In the early hours of 16 April 1941 the German Luftwaffe dropped an incendiary device on Masham. The bomb partially destroyed the White Boar Inn and killed two couples. Today a monument with a brass plaque stands in memory of those who lost their lives on that night.

MALHAM COVE

A visitor to Malham Cove in the 18th century described this natural beauty spot as... 'This beautiful rock is like the age-tinted wall of a prodigious castle; the stone is very white, and from the ledges hang various shrubs and vegetables, which with the tints given it by the

This is the delightful Monk Bridge in the village of Malham, which has long been popular with painters and photographers. It was built in 1636, but it has been subsequently widened.

bog water and c. gives it a variety that I never before saw so pleasing in a plain rock...' A television series in 2005 called *Seven Natural Wonders* described it as the 'wonder of Yorkshire'. One of the main features of the cove is the massive curved cliff face made from limestone. The cliff is approximately 80 metres high and 300 metres wide and on a bright sunny day, when the sunlight shines off the white rock, one cannot fail but to stand in awe at this majestic sight, for Malham Cove is truly a powerful symbol of the ruggedness of the North.

It was at the end of the last Ice Age, about 10,000 years ago, when the cove and the valley was formed. As the glacier melted a large waterfall was created over the cliff and it is thought that it might once have been equal to that of Niagara Falls. Although this may never be proved for certain, there can be no question that an astounding volume of water must have flowed over this waterfall to carve out such a stupendous feature. Today the waterfall has gone and the last time water flowed over it to any great extent was in the early 19th century following a period of prolonged heavy rain.

It has been the inspiration for many artists and writers, and Charles Kingsley, who was a regular visitor to Malham, wrote part of his book *The Water Babies* here. Gordale Scar runs for over a mile and can be considered as North Yorkshire's very own Grand Canyon.

Another interesting feature of the cove is the limestone pavement, which is made up of blocks of limestone called 'clints' and the gaps between them that are called 'grykes'. The pavement is found at the top of the cliff and can be reached by steps, which although a steep climb is well worth it as it offers breathtaking views of the dale towards the village of Malham and beyond. It is easy to see why this place has been so popular with visitors for centuries. Interestingly, the name Malham is derived from the Old Norse word *malgum* and means a 'gravely place', which is an apt name, for this dramatic landscape is full of hidden dangers and should be approached with diligence and respect.

The 'clints' and 'grykes' on top of Malham Cove.

Malham Tarn.

MALHAM TARN

There is evidence that the area was inhabited as far back as the Mesolithic era (also known as the Middle Stone Age), when primitive hunters would camp on the banks of the Tarn while on hunting trips. During the Bronze and Iron ages man began to take up a more permanent residence and began to farm the surrounding land. As the land was harsh, it would be more favourable to pastoral farming than agricultural.

Malham Tarn is a glacial lake, which was formed when the glaciers began to melt at the end of the last Ice Age about 10,000 years ago. It is the highest lake in England at 1,240 feet above sea level and is located in the Malham and Arncliffe Site of Special Scientific Interest. The Tarn is an upland alkaline lake, of which there are only eight in Europe.

The area was once owned by the monasteries, but following the Dissolution in the 16th century the estates of Malham Moor changed hands a number of times. Eventually, in the 18th century the lands were acquired by Thomas Lister, 1st Lord Ribblesdale. In the 1780s he built a hunting lodge on the site of an old farm, and in 1852 the estate was sold to James Morrison, a businessman and Member of Parliament. A number of important visitors stayed at Malham Tarn House, including John Ruskin and Charles Darwin.

Today the house is run as the Malham Tarn Field Studies Centre, and is rented to the Field Studies Council by the National Trust.

JANET'S FOSS

Janet's Foss (also known as Jennet's Foss) is located near to Gordale Scar and is thought to be named after the queen of the local fairies, who it is said lives in a cave behind the falls. In former times, the pool below the waterfall was used to wash sheep prior to shearing in June. While the sheep were driven into the pool, men would stand up to their chests in the water waiting to wash them. Even though it was summer the water was bitterly cold and the men wrapped themselves in sacking and drank strong liquor in an attempt to keep warm.

West Tanfield is famous for being one of the most picturesque villages in Yorkshire and is a popular beauty spot among tourists.

Janet's Foss.

Nearby can be found Janet's cave, which is a different cave from the one which she was thought to dwell in. This cave was once inhabited by smelters who were working at the mines on Pikedaw Hill.

GORDALE SCAR

Another dramatic and foreboding feature to be found in the district is the awesome Gordale Scar. This spectacular gorge cuts deep into the limestone hillside and was created by the melt-water from the receding glaciers. It is thought that it could be as much as 16 million years old. Initially, the water formed a cavern, but over the millennia the roof collapsed leaving the gaping gorge, complete with waterfalls. It is a popular place for painters and photographers. In 1814 James Ward finished his painting of Gordale Scar, which had been commissioned by Lord Ribblesdale, who owned the Scar. This gigantic painting, which measured an incredible 4.2 by 3.3 metres, is described as being possibly the best landscape painting ever painted. Sadly, the painter's

Harrogate's coat of arms.

career was brought to an end when he suffered a stroke in 1855 and he died in poverty four years later.

HARROGATE

The delightful town of Harrogate even today has the well-deserved reputation of a place of genteel elegance. It was William Slingsby who was to put Harrogate on the map in the late 16th century, for prior to that it had been no more than a sleepy hamlet. In 1571 William had been out riding when he observed a flock of lapwings drinking from a spring. His mouth dry from the ride, he decided to slake his thirst there. William was well travelled and had taken the waters in the spa towns on the Continent and on taking a sip of the spring water he was astonished to discover that it tasted remarkably similar to the mineral waters he had drunk there. A well was built at the spot and was to become known as the Tewit Well (Tewit being the local name for lapwings). Although it is generally accepted that this was the beginning of Harrogate's association with the spa, it was renowned for the health-giving properties of its waters hundreds of years earlier than this.

*The dramatic
Gordale Scar.*

Tewit Well: built on the spot where William Slingsby discovered the mineral qualities of Harrogate's water in the late 16th century.

Along the present day Cold Bath Road can be found a small strip of grass where the well of St Mungo once stood. He lived locally in about 512. He was renowned for his cures, especially on children.

Originally Harrogate was two small villages: High Harrogate and Low Harrogate, which were located on the edge of the old forest of Knaresborough. Its name is thought to derive from Anglo-Saxon 'Haywra-gate' meaning 'the road that passes near the corner of an enclosure'.

The waters of Harrogate are known as 'juvenile' or 'plutonic', which means that the wells are fed from sources deep in the earth's crust and not from rainfall. These deep springs permeate through the rocks, which impart their mineral qualities to the waters. Harrogate can boast the world's biggest diversity of different types of mineral waters to be found in any one area.

In 1626 Dr Edmund Deane published his book – *Spadacrene Anglica OR, THE ENGLISH SPAWFOVNTAINE. BEING A BRIEFE TREATISE of the acide, or tart Fountaine in the Forest of Knaresborow, in the West-Riding* of Yorkshire. As also a Relation of other medicinall Waters in the said Forest.*

Harrogate's famous 'Stray'.

The Crown Hotel.

*It should be noted that Harrogate was once in the West Riding of Yorkshire; however, after 1974, with the enactment of the Local Government Act of 1972, it became part of North Yorkshire.

According to the good doctor, in chapter 14 of his work, the best time to take the waters was in the morning and one should drink it sparingly, perhaps increasing the quantity daily by degrees. He goes on to say that if one has a good stomach then drinking it twice a day may be advantageous.

Edmund was born near Halifax to Gilbert and Elizabeth Deane. He had three brothers, Gilbert, Richard and Symon (who was his twin). The actual date of his birth is unknown; however, his entry of baptism records it as 23 March 1572. It appears that his mother died while giving birth to the boys or shortly after, for the date of her funeral is two days later. Edmund entered Merton College, Oxford, where he matriculated on 26 March 1591 and obtained his bachelor's degree on 11 December

1594. On 28 March 1601 he became licensed to practise medicine.

After completing his studies he moved to York where he practised medicine until his death in 1640. Nothing is known about his life in this fair city, except that he was to occupy a house on a street called Pavement, which was where criminals were punished and a permanent pillory had been erected for this purpose. It is not, therefore, unreasonable to conclude that the good doctor had chosen this site to practise so that he could administer to

A crown and floral display outside the Crown Hotel.

these wretched souls. This fact can be attested by his leaving a legacy in his will for the provision of the prisoners. He was buried in St Crux Church, York, but the church was demolished in 1885 after it was considered structurally unsound. Sadly, there are no memorials to him and his name does not appear in the parish register as records were only kept after 1678. So we are left with only his book on the waters of Harrogate as a memorial to Dr Edmund Deane.

The first public bathing house was built in 1663, but by the end of the century there were a total of 20. Although High Harrogate was considered the more fashionable, a number of hotels were built in Low Harrogate, the Crown Hotel being the oldest. It is thought that it was old even when Joseph Thackwray purchased it in 1740. Initially it had been a small inn, but its close proximity to the famous sulphur well resulted in it soon expanding into an important hotel, renowned for the quality of its accommodation. Among its famous guests was

Lord Byron, who stayed there in 1806. In 1835 the great-nephew of Thackwray, who was also called Joseph, courted controversy when he sunk his own well close to the sulphur well. However, in 1837 at a hearing at York Assizes he agreed to give it up for public use.

At the beginning of the 18th century the future of Harrogate Spa seemed doubtful with the passing of an Act of Parliament, which decreed the enclosure of the Royal Forest. In 1778, however, the Stray was created by the Enclosure Act. This consisted of an area of 200 acres of open parkland. Its size was fixed by the Act, and even to this day if a part should be removed, for whatever purpose, it must be replaced elsewhere. During the 19th century part of the Stray was used as a racecourse; however, it should be noted that this is no longer possible, for the 1985 Harrogate Stray Act prevents the racing of horses, or indeed any other animal, on this land.

The Promenade Room was built in 1806 and is the oldest of Harrogate's spa buildings still

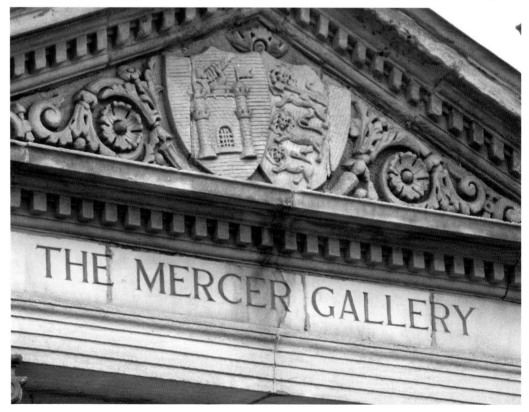

Detail of the pediment above the main entrance of the Promenade Room. It now houses the Mercer Art Gallery.

The Royal Pump Room, built in 1842.

standing. Today, it houses the Mercer Art Gallery, but the property has had a number of uses, including as a theatre, where some very famous Victorian names performed, including Oscar Wilde and Lily Langtry. By the end of the 1830s at least 10,000 people were visiting Harrogate each year. Not all visitors, however, found the place to their liking and in 1858, after visiting the town, Charles Dickens wrote, 'Harrogate is the queerest place with the strangest people in it, leading the oddest lives of dancing, newspaper reading and dining.'

Far left: A doorway to the Royal Pump Room.

Left: ARX CELEBTIS FONTIBUS – 'A town famous for its water'. The town's coat of arms and motto.

Hales Bar: a 17th-century coaching inn.

inn. It has been known by a number of names; after the opening of the nearby Promenade Room it became the Promenade Inn and in 1862 it adopted the name of its landlord, William Hale. During the 1950s and 1960s it became a favourite bar of Sir John Barbirolli, when visiting each summer with the Halle Orchestra.

In 1860, with the opening of Victoria Avenue, the two villages of High and Low Harrogate were finally joined together to form the town. At one time this avenue had private entrance gates. The development consisted of a number of elegant buildings, wide roads and pavements, trees and grass verges.

The introduction of a railway network increased the popularity of the town and by the end of the 1860s it received about 30,000 visitors each year. In 1842 the Royal Pump Room, designed by I.T. Shutt, was built over the old sulphur well, and its basement was noted for having eight wells. Across the road from the Pump Room stands Hales Bar, which was established in the 17th century as a coaching

In 1919 Fredrick Belmont opened the doors for the first time to the now world-famous Bettys Tea Rooms. But the story started many years earlier in the small Swiss village of Wangen-an-der-Aare. On 20 December 1890 a fire broke out in the local mill, which was owned by Fredrick's father Johann Bützer, the master baker. As soon as the fire was discovered

One of the delightful streets of the genteel Harrogate.

Johann grabbed young Fritz, aged five, and his sister Ida, aged seven, and took them to safety, while his wife Karolina carried the two babies out of the burning mill. Once outside, however, Johann realised that his eldest daughter Rosalia was still inside the building. Without a thought for his own safety and braving the flames, he rushed back into the mill. Tragically, they were both to perish in the conflagration. Until the age of 14 Fritz worked for a farmer, at which time he left to train as a baker, like his father before him.

Over the next few years he moved from job to job, and working his way round Switzerland and France he eventually arrived in London, where he promptly lost his entire luggage. It was here that an old man took pity on him and put him into a cab back to the railway station, where he boarded a train bound for Yorkshire. After arriving at Bradford he initially found work with a fellow Swiss confectioner called Bonnet and it was at this time that he changed his name to Fredrick Belmont and styled himself as a chocolate specialist. In 1912 the renowned toffee producers Farrah's invited him to Harrogate.

The beautiful Yorkshire countryside, with its wonderfully clear air, reminded Belmont so much of Switzerland that he decided to make it his home. The opening of Bettys Tea Rooms proved an instant success, and soon Fredrick had also added a craft bakery to his growing business empire. This paved the way for other branches to be opened throughout Yorkshire. During World War Two his tea rooms in York became very popular with the American and Canadian aircrews, who were stationed around the city. Many of these servicemen left an indelible reminder of those far-off days as they signed their names with a diamond pen on to a mirror, which can still be seen in Bettys at York.

In the 1960s the company joined forces with another famous family business – Taylors of Harrogate. Taylors was founded in 1866 by Charles and Llewellyn Taylor. Charles had started his career buying and blending teas for grocers in the south-west of England – grocers

Bettys Tea Rooms.

The elegant entrance to the shop selling the famous 'Harrogate Toffee'.

who would then sell these as their own blends. After losing his job after making an extremely risky purchase, Charles decided to go into partnership with his brother. So, in 1866, the two brothers opened a small warehouse in Leeds as C.E. Taylor and Co. With Charles's flair for creating tea blends, which were especially suited to local water, the business soon took off. It was to become even more successful after they opened several kiosk coffee houses. Another famous company with its roots in the town is Farrah's of Harrogate. Founded in 1840 by John Farrah, the Original Harrogate Toffee was created to clear one's palate of the strong foul-tasting sulphur water.

RIPLEY CASTLE

At the heart of the delightful village of Ripley is the castle, which has been owned by the Ingilby family ever since Sir Thomas Ingleby (1290–1352) married Edeline Thwenge in 1308. (Over time the spelling of surnames often changed. This was not an uncommon practice and for many centuries people were known to spell their names in a variety of ways. Little importance was attached to the spelling of a name; it was the name itself that was important.) The castle and estates were her substantial dowry. It proved not to be a happy century for the inhabitants of Ripley Castle and the village, for in 1318 the region was brutally plundered by the Scots. This was followed by an outbreak of bovine plague, which all but wiped out the cattle in the district, reducing many families to destitution and creating a severe shortage of milk. But it was the Black Death of 1348 which would have the most disastrous consequences for the population. With nearly half of the country wiped out due to this pestilence, many villages and hamlets simply vanished. Although Ripley managed to survive,

Ripley Castle.

A door knocker at Ripley Castle with the Ingilby family crest.

the old village was abandoned and the survivors built their new one next to the castle.

In 1357 Sir Thomas's eldest son (also called Thomas) saved the life of Edward III while they were hunting in the Forest of Knaresborough. The king had thrown his spear at a wild boar, but it had only injured the beast. The boar, maddened by its wound, charged at the king, which unseated the sovereign and he was thrown to the ground. Acting quickly, Thomas came to the king's rescue and despatched the angry creature, thereby saving Edward's life. Grateful for his subject's prompt actions, Edward knighted Thomas and granted the right for the family to show a boar's head on their crest. He also granted the village the right to hold a weekly market and an annual horse fair: both being held until the early 1900s. In the centre of the village stands a drinking well with a boar mounted on top, which was presented by the Hon. Alicia-Margaret Ingilby in 1907.

Sir William Ingleby (1518–1578), although married to a staunch Catholic, would be handsomely rewarded for his loyalty to the Crown following the failed Pilgrimage of Grace. During his journey south to be crowned James

I of England the Scottish king was entertained at Ripley Castle. His host Sir William Ingleby (1546–1618) would, only two years later, be implicated in the Gunpowder Plot, being either related to or closely associated with nine of the principal conspirators. Remarkably, after being arrested and charged with treason, Sir William and his son were acquitted of all charges.

The Inglebys were loyal supporters of Charles I throughout the Civil War, and fought under Prince Rupert of the Rhine. At the Battle of Marston Moor Sir William Ingleby (1594–1652) fought alongside his spirited sister 'Trooper' Jane Ingleby. After the battle they both made it safely back to the castle, but almost as soon as they were home Oliver Cromwell arrived. Sir William promptly hid in the priest hole, leaving his sister to deal with the unwelcome visitor. At first she refused entry to the victorious general, but after negotiations Cromwell was allowed to stay the night. It is doubtful though that he would have spent a comfortable repose, for Jane guarded him the entire time with a loaded pistol. Having just won the greatest victory of his career, this

The Weeping Cross in the churchyard at Ripley. It is thought that it was used by pilgrims and penitents, and that the grooves in the base were for their knees. It is the only known example of its type in England.

This drinking fountain was presented to the inhabitants of Ripley by the Honourable Alicia Margaret Dame Ingilby in 1907.

treatment must have come as something of a shock to him. The next morning she showed him off the premises. But while this small if slightly amusing drama was being played out by a very brave lady, events of a more sinister and unpleasant nature were being carried out just a few hundred yards away. On the east wall of the church are a number of marks which were created by Parliamentarian soldiers as they executed Royalist prisoners following the battle.

Today, the castle and estate are still owned by the Ingilbys, a family which has been at the forefront of English history for nearly 700 years.

RIPON

The history of the cathedral city of Ripon stretches back into Neolithic times as the great number of earthworks and henges which are to be found in the district attest. There is evidence of Roman occupation of the area, as in the 19th century a quantity of coins and samples of pottery were unearthed.

The Venerable Bede referred to the settlement as Inhrypum, and over time it has been called Hrypsaetna, Onhripum, Rhypum, Hryppum, Hrypon, Rhypon, Ripium, Ripum

and Rippon. During the early 19th century the second 'p' was dropped and its present spelling was obtained. Its name is derived from the name of a tribe, Hrype, who were thought to have settled here during the sixth century.

In 672 St Wilfrid constructed his church at Ripon. To produce his wonderful stone edifice he brought in the best stonemasons, plasterers and glaziers from France and Italy. The eighth-century priest called Eddius Stephanus (Stephen of Ripon) wrote in his book on the life of St Wilfrid, *Vita Sancti Wilfridi,* that the church was built completely from dressed stone and supported by various columns. It had many windows, arched vaults, a winding cloister and was of a great height.

Sadly, this great basilica was totally destroyed by King Eadred in 948 as an example to Archbishop Wulfstan of York after his part in a Northumbrian uprising: the only part of the church to survive was the seventh-century crypt. Shortly after the destruction of St Wildrid's magnificent structure a new minster was erected. This was later destroyed by William

A statue of Thurstan, the Archbishop of York.
(By kind permission of the Chapter of Ripon Cathedral).

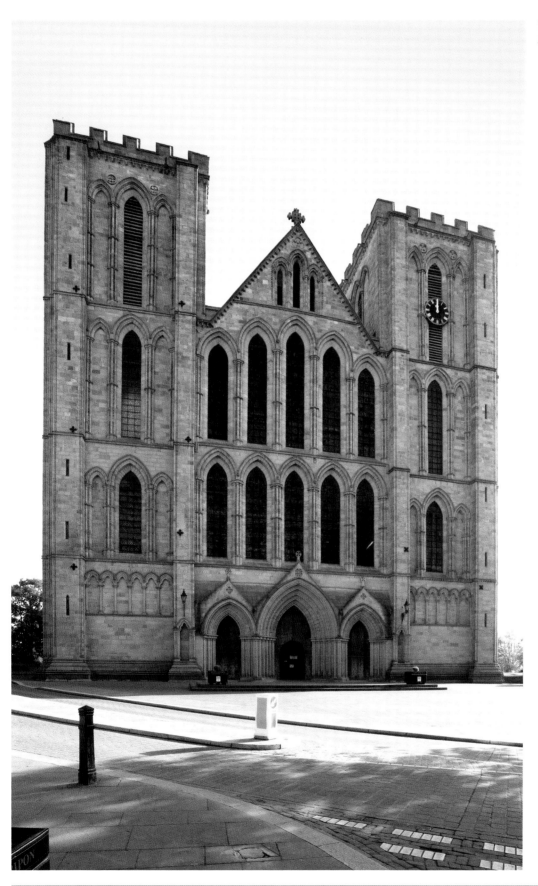

The outstanding Ripon Cathedral.

The fabulous choir stalls.
(By kind permission of the Chapter of Ripon Cathedral).

A misericord (sometimes known as a mercy seat) is a small wooden shelf, which was installed so that those monks who were either old or infirm could get some relief during the long periods of standing while praying. It comes from the Latin word 'misericordia' which literally means 'act of mercy'. It is said that it is the carving on this particular misericord which inspired the Mad March Hare in Lewis Carroll's Alice's Adventures in Wonderland.
(By kind permission of the Chapter of Ripon Cathedral).

The hand moves up and down to tell the choir when to sit and stand.
(By kind permission of the Chapter of Ripon Cathedral).

the Conqueror in 1069. A third church was built on the orders of Thomas of Bayeux, the first Norman Archbishop of York, and evidence of this church can still be found in the present cathedral. In the 12th century Archbishop Roger de Pont L'Evêque funded the construction of a grand minster. This stunning minster finally became a cathedral in 1836.

In 1108 Ripon was granted the right to hold a market, which is still held each Thursday in the square. Originally, the market was administered by the church. At 11 o'clock each Thursday the bellman rings his bell to announce that the market is open; this tradition goes back to when the city had a corn market which was opened in this way.

At 9 o'clock each night an ancient custom is maintained when the wakeman blows his horn at the obelisk in the market square. This signals that he is on duty and the city is now safely in his hands and those of his constables. The custom has been continuously performed for over 1,000 years, and it is said that it dates back to 886, when Alfred the Great granted the town its first charter.

During the Middle Ages the wakeman was selected from 12 aldermen, and would serve for a 12-month period. Those who refused to accept the office would be punished by a heavy fine. The wakeman was responsible for apprehending criminals and also for paying compensation to their victims. For this service, each householder of the town would pay two pence for every outer door to their buildings, which they would pay once a year.

During World War One Ripon was the location of one of the largest army camps in the country, which accommodated close to 30,000 troops. For a time the famous war poet Wilfred Owen was stationed here, and it was during his stay that he wrote some of his best and most-loved poetry.

KNARESBOROUGH

The delightful market town of Knaresborough lays claim to having the oldest chemist's shop in England, which dates back to 1720. It is thought that the pharmacy trade began here as far back as the 13th century. The town is also famous for its ruined castle. Dating from the 14th century,

The Ripon Gazette: this building once served as the borough police station (1875–1887). An extension was built at the rear of the building which housed four police cells.

The Cabman's Shelter was provided through a legacy of £200 by Sarah Carter, a former mayor's daughter, in 1911. This rare structure was built by Boulton and Paul of Norwich and gave shelter to the cabmen while they waited for fares in the market place.

The Town Hall was designed by James Wyatt in 1798. Originally it housed the public assembly and reading rooms. In 1897 the Marquess of Ripon gave it to the city to be used as the Town Hall.

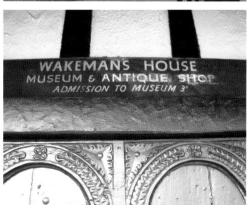

The Wakeman's House.

Far Left: Knaresborough Bridge spanning the River Nidd.

Right: The oldest chemist's shop in England, which is located in Knaresborough.

Far right: Old Mother Shipton.

it was built on the site of a previous castle, which had been constructed by a baron called Serlo de Burg in Norman times. In 1399 Richard II was imprisoned within the walls of this castle until he was moved to Pontefract Castle, where he was murdered on 14 February 1400. It was also Knaresborough Castle where the murderers of Thomas Becket sought refuge, hiding there for three years after committing their heinous crime in 1170.

During a violent storm in 1488 the famous witch, Mother Shipton, was born. It is said that her birth was accompanied by eerie screams and Agatha, her mother, expired during the ordeal. The girl was called Ursula Southeil and her childhood was filled with mysterious and

inexplicable events. In 1512 she married Tony Shipton. She was thought by many to be a witch and her crooked facial features did nothing to allay their suspicions. She is best remembered for her predictions and, of course, her cave and the dropping well with its petrifying qualities. The well was described in the early 16th century by John Leland.

Right: Knaresborough Castle.

Far right: Blind Jack.

Carved out of the rock above the River Nidd is St Robert's Cave. It was the home of a local hermit called Robert Flower, who is thought to have lived an exceptionally long life from 1116 to 1218. As well as his remarkable longevity, Robert was credited with the gift of healing. St Robert's Cave is also known as Eugene Aram's Cave. In 1745 the schoolteacher Eugene Aram murdered Daniel Clark, a local shoemaker, and hid his body in this cave. The story is told in Edward Bulmer-Lytton's novel written in 1832.

In 1408 a local stonemason called John carved a chapel out of the rock. He built this shrine in thanksgiving for his son, who had miraculously escaped with his life after nearly being crushed to death by falling rocks. John had been working in a nearby quarry while his son had been playing by the rock face and a sudden fall of boulders narrowly missed the young boy. The stonemason, convinced that his son had been saved by the intervention of the Virgin Mary, constructed this shrine and dedicated it to her. Our Lady of the Crag is thought to be the third oldest wayside shrine in

Britain. At the entrance to the shrine is a large carving of a knight drawing his sword; his identity is unknown, but the carving is thought to be very old.

Another famous inhabitant of Knaresborough was John Metcalf (1717–1810), better known as Blind Jack. Even though he lost his sight at the age of six from smallpox, he went on to achieve many remarkable things, including fighting on the Hanoverian side at Falkirk and Culloden in 1746. He was also a musician, forest guide and smuggler; but it is his road construction for which he will be remembered the most, and he is regarded as the first of Britain's modern road builders.

FOUNTAINS ABBEY

In 1132 a number of the monks at St Mary's Abbey in York were beginning to feel uneasy about the relaxed way of life that had become prevalent among their community. They wished to return to the strict Rules of St Benedict and a much more austere existence, which they thought more befitting a monastery, and one that the abbey had followed in earlier times. Six monks approached the prior for his advice and discovered that he was in total agreement with them. Prior Richard readily agreed to go to the abbot and put their case before him. The abbot, who was called Geoffrey, was an old man and set in his ways. He viewed this as a betrayal of the faith and a flagrant attack on his authority.

The discussions dragged on over the summer months, but nothing was resolved. Meanwhile the group of dissident monks had grown to 13 in number. Realising that the abbot was intransigent, Richard appealed directly to Archbishop Thurstan, who was a personal friend of his. Thurstan decided that he should visit the abbey to resolve the matter. When he arrived, however, a fight broke out in the cloisters when monks loyal to the abbot shamefully attempted to bar the archbishop and his officials from entering the chapter house. Thurstan quickly led the 13 monks into the church, where he barred the door for their safety.

Under his protection, he took the monks to his house, where they were to stay for the next couple of months. As Christmas approached they went with him to his collegiate church in Ripon, where they celebrated the festival. On 27 December 1132 he took them to some wasteland a few miles from Ripon in the narrow valley of the River Skell. It was here that they were to stay and establish their new abbey. They were to give the abbey its name from the springs of water which flowed from the rocky sides of the valley – Fountains.

At first life for these monks was harsh in the extreme, for they had nowhere to shelter during the bitter winter months except beneath the rocks. The land had not been inhabited for centuries and was overgrown with coarse thorns. It was more befitting for wild animals, rather than a group of men, but their zeal and determination far outweighed any adversity which was presented to them. So these holy men set about taming and clearing the land in preparation for their future abbey.

The monks decided that Prior Richard should be their leader and duly elected him as their first abbot (of the 13 monks who founded the abbey, eight became abbots and one even became a saint). With only the clothes on their backs and a store of bread, which had been provided by Archbishop Thurstan, they set about building their community. They now had the added problem that they belonged to no particular order. It was decided that they should approach the Cistercian Order, which they had long admired. The abbey was accepted by the Cistercians and became the daughter house of the Abbey of Clairvaux in Burgundy. An experienced monk from Clairvaux, called Geoffrey d'Ainai, along with a number of fellow monks, travelled to Yorkshire to instruct the new abbey in the Cistercian way.

Life at Fountains would remain difficult for the monks over the next few years, and they would come to near starvation on more than one occasion. At one point they were so desperate that they had to survive on a gruel which had been made from elm leaves. The fragile existence of the fledgling community had suffered through the lack of outside support, but in 1135 they were able to see the faint glimmer of light at the end of the tunnel, as Hugh, Dean of York, retired to the abbey and brought with him his library and substantial wealth. Serlo and Tosti, who were canons of York, followed the example of the dean and joined the abbey. This meant that the abbey now enjoyed some financial security.

Work on the stone structure of the abbey did not start until the end of the 1130s. In 1147 a fire interrupted construction, but not for long, for shortly afterwards work resumed. Building work to complete the monastery gradually went on for over half a century. It was, however, to receive numerous alterations and additions over the centuries, especially in the early 13th century when John of Kent, who was an insatiable builder, was abbot.

During the Middle Ages it was common practice to use acoustic jars in the construction of European churches. Their use is thought to be based on the ideas of the Roman architect, Vitravius, who stated that the use of resonant jars in amphitheatres would greatly improve the clarity of the voice. Excavations carried out in the 19th century at Fountains Abbey have revealed a masonry-lined pit on either side of the choir. These pits had recesses in the masonry which held acoustic jars to give more resonance to the singing of the choir. Today one of these jars may be viewed in the abbey museum.

By the latter part of the 13th century the abbey was one of the most powerful in the north and the richest Cistercian house in England. Unfortunately, its fortunes were to fluctuate wildly and it faced crisis and controversy on many occasions. In 1274 the abbey was £900 in debt to moneylenders and the king was forced to appoint a commissioner to administer the monastery's affairs. By 1291, however, their debt had risen to an astounding £6,373 and once again the king was compelled to step in and appoint another commissioner. The abbey's money problems were brought about by the common practice of pre-selling their wool for substantial payments in advance. This was a risky business, but it brought in desperately needed funds and, if production was good, it was a gamble which paid off. But when the quality and the quantity fell short of what had been expected, the abbey would fall into debt. In 1280 an epidemic of sheep-scab had caused a number of lean years in the production of wool.

The abbey was to operate for just over 400 years and was finally abandoned in 1539 during the Dissolution of the Monasteries. On 1 October 1540 it was sold by the Crown to Sir Richard Gresham, a merchant from London. In 1597 it was sold by the Greshams to Stephen Proctor, who built Fountains Hall in 1616 using stone which was taken from the abbey. After he died the abbey passed through several hands until in 1768 it was bought by William Aislabie. He incorporated the ruined edifice into the ornamental grounds of Studley Royal, which had been started by his father, John Aislabie, Chancellor of the Exchequer, in 1717. Today Fountains Abbey, the Hall and Studley Royal are all owned by the National Trust.

SETTLE

In about the seventh century AD Anglo-Saxon settlers arrived in the area and established a settlement on the banks of the River Ribble. The name Settle is derived from Old English and means a 'dwelling' or a 'house'. Over time these settlers were displaced as Norse-Irish migrants moved into the area; they had been descended from earlier Viking invasions of Ireland.

Ye Olde Naked Man in Settle.

There are a number of caves in the district which show that there was human activity in the area going back well into prehistoric times. Perhaps the most notable of these is the Victoria Cave, so named because the inner chamber was discovered in 1837 on the day of Queen Victoria's accession to the throne. In the cave were found the remains of animals which have long since vanished from these islands, such as bears, reindeer, hippopotami, mammoths, elephants and even the sabre-toothed tiger. Among these remarkable finds were discovered flints, which would not naturally be found in this region. It is therefore clear that these would have been brought here for the sole purpose of producing arrowheads and other implements. It is also thought that the cave was occupied in about 450 by Romano-British refugees while escaping from early Anglo-Saxon raiders.

Even by the late 11th century, it is clear by its entry in the *Domesday Book* that Settle was still only sparsely populated. In 1249 Henry III granted the town the right to hold a market each Tuesday: this was a charter obtained by the lord of the manor, Henry de Percy (1228–1272).

The market is still held every Tuesday, but livestock is no longer sold there.

By the time of the Industrial Revolution in the late 18th century the town had become a centre for the spinning of cotton. A number of earlier mills which had originally been constructed to grind corn were converted for cotton spinning. According to the journalist Edward Baines (1774–1843) in his book *History of the Cotton Manufacture in Great Britain*, which he wrote in 1835, Settle had five cotton mills and employed 333 people.

In the centre of Settle stands a large impressive building called the Folly. This edifice was constructed in 1679 by Richard Preston, a wealthy local tanner, and originally the building was called Tanner Hall. After he died in 1695 it passed to his daughter Margaret, who sold it to the Dawsons, a wealthy local family, whose descendants were to own the property until 1980. Over the years it has had a variety of uses,

including a bakery, a warehouse, and even a fish and chip shop.

After it was sold in 1980 it was used by an antique dealer for a number of years, until it was purchased by a property developer. The developer abandoned its plans and it was put on the market in 1990. It failed to attract any buyers and was divided into two houses in 1994. Parts of the building were unoccupied and subsequently began to deteriorate. Fortunately, the North Craven Building Preservation Trust stepped in and campaigned for the rescue of this magnificent property. This remarkable Grade I listed building is unusual in that its architecture belongs predominantly to one period, which is that of the late 17th century.

Another famous feature in the town is Ye Olde Naked Man Cafe, which was once a public house: it is so named because of the figure on the front of the building, who holds a board in front of him with the year 1663 on it. The more

The Folly in Settle.

The Hoffman kiln at Langcliffe near Settle.

observant will notice that the man is wearing what appear to be riding boots and there are the faintest outlines of buttons on his chest: so perhaps he is not so naked after all.

Located just outside of Settle at Langcliffe is a remarkable Hoffman Kiln. This gem of our industrial past is unique in Britain. This type of kiln was first patented in Danzig by a German called Friedrich Hoffman in 1858. Originally, it was designed for the firing of bricks, but it was later used for the burning of lime. It was known as the 'Hoffman Continuous Kiln'. The kiln at Langcliffe was built in 1872 and would remain in continuous use until 1931, with the exception of one short period in 1926 when it was closed during industrial action. During World War Two the kiln was used to store chemicals. When English Heritage identified the kiln as being the best example of a Hoffman kiln still standing in Britain they were also to schedule it as an ancient monument.

During its working life the kiln produced lime of a very high quality, which had many industrial uses, including tanning, water softening, sugar refining and the production of perfume and chocolate. The conditions which the workers endured at the kiln were harsh and unpleasant and the work was extremely intensive. Over time the kiln became uneconomical to run, especially as industrial reliance on lime reduced to such an extent that it was no longer viable to keep the kiln at Langcliffe open. The kiln chimney was demolished in the 1950s. It was first weakened, and the press and TV crews were invited to watch the spectacle; however, to their disappointment they arrived too late, for it collapsed during the night.

CLAPHAM

The village of Clapham is located at the foot of Ingleborough, and is a well-known starting point for the ascent of the mountain. Its name is derived from the Old English words 'clœpe' and 'ham', meaning 'homestead by the noisy stream'. Records show that there has been a church there since at least 1160. However, the original church, along with the rest of the village, was burnt to the ground during a raid in the early 14th century by the Scots, following

Brokken Bridge at Clapham.

their decisive victory at the Battle of Bannockburn (24 June 1314). Although the present church dates from the 19th century, it is thought that the tower was erected shortly after this Scottish raid.

Running through the village is Clapham Beck, which starts its journey as the Fell Beck, high upon the slopes of Ingleborough. The Fell Beck drops into Gaping Gill, which is England's highest waterfall and falls 110 metres into the pothole. It eventually emerges via Ingleborough Cave into Clapham Beck. The village has a total of four bridges, two of which are footbridges called Brokken Bridge and Mafeking Bridge.

In 1947 a grisly discovery was made in a cave above the village: the Trow Ghyll skeleton. It was found by two keen potholers – Jim Leach from Blackburn and Harold Burgess from Leeds. They were good friends and both members of the Northern Pennine Club (one of the oldest and largest caving clubs in the UK). They had been searching for new potholes to explore and just after midday they discovered a small hole which was partly hidden by loose stones. After clearing away the stones, Jim began to climb down to explore the cave. He had not gone more than 10 feet when he saw a pair of shoes. It was then that he discovered the badly decomposed remains of a man. His partner found a small bottle of white powder lying near to the body, which they assumed to be flash powder (later forensic testing revealed that the substance was sodium cyanide – a lethal poison).

A post-mortem was unable to shed any light on the cause of death. Although it was possible it could have been from the poison, the bottle was full. During the examination they managed to ascertain that the body was of a male between the age of 22 and 30, and five feet five and half inches tall, but his identity was never discovered. Some maintained that he was a German spy, and certainly, as his death had occurred between two and six years before, placing it sometime during World War Two, it was a theory not without some foundation. Among his possessions was found a key; unfortunately, the police were never able to identify the lock to which it belonged. Whoever he was, it was a secret which he was to take to the grave.

REGINALD JOHN FARRER (1880–1920)

In the 18th century the Farrer family made Clapham their residence and created their Ingleborough estate there. Reginald John Farrer was born into this wealthy family. His early education was conducted at home due to his speech defect, which had been caused by a number of operations on a cleft palate. It was while being taught at home that he developed his lifelong passion for high places and the mountain plants which inhabited them. By the time he was 10 he was already an experienced field botanist, and at 14 he created his first rock garden, in a disused quarry on the family estate.

At the age of 17 he entered Oxford University, and while there he was to be instrumental in the creation of a rock garden at St John's College. After graduation he embarked on his first expedition to Eastern Asia, where he spent some time in China, Korea and Japan. It was during his eight-month stay in Japan that he developed his strong views on rock garden design. These were greatly influenced by the Japanese aesthetics of gardening, which had initially developed from their Shinto beliefs. Originally little more than open spaces of gravel intended to encourage the spirits, or kami, to visit, over time rocks and trees were added (in the belief that kami inhabited these places). But it was during the Kamakura period in Japan, from 1185 to 1333, that the Zen Buddhists greatly influenced the art of garden design. Farrar was drawn to the clean lines and apparent simplicity of these gardens.

Upon his return to England he initially tried his hand at writing poetry and novels, but it soon became obvious to him that his strength lay in gardens and writing about them. His book *My Rock Garden*, which was published in 1907, became very popular and was continuously reprinted for the next 40 years.

During his relatively short life Farrer was an avid traveller and collector of plants. Although he wrote a number of books, it was his first book *My Rock Garden* which was to remain the most popular (though it is sadly now long out of print). He was also to receive the accolade of having a number of plants named after him. It was while on his last expedition to Upper Burma that he died alone in the remote Minshan Mountains: it is thought that he had contracted diphtheria. He was buried in Konglu, which is a town in north-east Burma. Farrer was a true English eccentric, who in the words of Nicola Shulman (his biographer) '…brought rock-gardening into the hearts of the British people.'

THE NORBER ERRATICS

During the last Ice Age glaciers scoured the landscape, dragging rocks and rubble and even great boulders until they were eventually deposited many miles from where they had originated. Not only did the glaciers shape and mould the landscape, but also, when they had melted, they left strangely positioned boulders, which we call 'erratics'. This is how a number of boulders located near Austwick found themselves on a hillside at Norber. These Norber Erratics were originally deposited on limestone, which over time has been dissolved by the rain and eroded by the wind. The limestone beneath the boulders has been protected, which has resulted in them now standing on pillars. In some cases the pillars of limestone reach 60cm in height. Walking around the Norber Erratics it is hard to believe that they are a totally natural phenomenon, and not the handiwork of some Neolithic man making his mark on the landscape.

SKIPTON

It is safe to say that the small North Yorkshire market town of Skipton would have started life as a sheep farm, for the name is derived from two Anglo-Saxon words 'scip' (sheep) and 'tun' (farm). In the *Domesday Book* it is recorded as Scipton. This delightful market town is also known as the 'Gateway to the Dales'. Little is known about its history prior to the Norman Conquest, but, we do know that it was under the control of an Anglo-Saxon earl named Edwin, who was killed during the uprising in 1070. After his death William the Conqueror took ownership of Skipton, and he later gave the estate to Robert de Romille, who had been one of his lieutenants.

The mid-12th century was a brutal time for the inhabitants of Skipton. King David of Scotland had despatched part of his army, under the command of William FitzDuncan, into Yorkshire to plunder and lay waste to the county. No one was spared from their savagery whether they were of high rank or low, male or female. Children were butchered before their

One of the stunning 'Erratics' at Norber.

parents, and people were stripped naked, tethered and cruelly tormented with the tips of swords. Cruelty was common, but even for the standards of the day this took barbarity to a new level.

In 1152 FitzDuncan became lord of the manor at Skipton and he married Alice de Romille; they had one son and three daughters (some sources maintain that they had two sons). According to tradition, their son, known as the Boy of Egremond, was tragically drowned in the treacherous waters of the Strid at Bolton Abbey. He had been out hunting with greyhounds, one of which he was holding with a leash. He came up to the Strid, which he had leapt many times before, so he was confident he could cross it with ease. As he leapt the greyhound refused to jump and pulled them both into the rapid waters. The dog managed to drag itself out, but the boy was not so lucky and his lifeless body was taken out of the river.

The town received its charter granting it the right to hold a market and an annual fair from King John in 1204. In 1548 William Ermysted founded a grammar school in the town for the instruction of boys.

In 1838 the moral philosopher Henry Sidgwick was born in Skipton. His father Reverend W. Sidgwick had been the headmaster of the grammar school. In 1859 Henry was elected a Fellow at Trinity College, Cambridge; he would also become a lecturer in the classics. He held this post for the next 10 years, after which time he changed to lecturing on moral philosophy. It was also at this time that he resigned his fellowship when he stated that, in good conscience, he could no longer declare himself a member of the Church of England. He would, however, retain his lectureship. In 1874 he published his major work called *The Methods of Ethics*. He was elected praelector on moral and political philosophy at Trinity in 1875, and eight years later he was elected

Knightbridge Professor of Philosophy: this, as well as being a senior professorship, was also one of the oldest, for the chair had been founded by John Knightbridge in 1683. In 1885 he was once again elected a Fellow of the college, after the religious test had been removed. He died on 28 August 1900.

Skipton was also the birthplace of an editor of *The Times* newspaper: George Geoffrey Dawson (1874–1974), who held the post in 1912 to 1919 and again from 1923 to 1941. Originally his surname had been Robinson, but he changed it in 1917. After Hitler had come to power in Germany Dawson became a strong supporter of the appeasement policies of Stanley Baldwin and Neville Chamberlain, and he would play a crucial role in the events which led to the Munich Agreement of 1938. He was a lifelong friend and regular dining companion of Edward Fox (Lord Halifax), who was another prominent appeaser. Dawson retired in 1941.

SKIPTON CASTLE

Skipton Castle was first built in 1090 by the Norman Baron Robert de Romille and originally it was constructed in the typical motte and bailey style of the time. It was necessary, however, to replace it shortly afterwards with a much more substantial stone structure, which was more capable of withstanding the frequent attacks from the north by the Scottish raiders.

In 1310 Robert Clifford took ownership of the property after it was granted to him by Edward II. Robert had been given the title of Lord Clifford and it had been created by writ that the title would pass through both the male and female lines of the family. The Cliffords had settled in England after the Norman Conquest. It had been Robert's intention to implement a number of improvements to the castle's fortifications, and although work had begun on these, he was killed at the Battle of Bannockburn in 1314 before they could be

completed. His son, Roger, born in 1299, joined the barons under Thomas, Earl of Lancaster, in their unsuccessful uprising against the king. As an example, 22 barons were executed and the Earl of Lancaster, along with six others (it did not seem fitting that a man as great and mighty as the earl should die alone), was hung, drawn and quartered. Roger, along with two other barons, was hanged in chains the following day at York, and the rest in various places in the realm.

It would be Lord John Clifford, born 8 April 1430, a Lancastrian supporter, who would carry out such a heinous act that his name would be forever stained by it and the infamy would be recorded for posterity by the pen of Shakespeare in *Henry VI*. He callously and cruelly murdered the helpless 17-year-old Edmund, Earl of Rutland, on old Wakefield Bridge, only steps away from the sanctuary of the chantry chapel. The young noble had been fleeing the battlefield with his tutor at the Battle of Wakefield in 1460. With the words 'thy father slew mine, and so will I thee, and all thy kin', Clifford plunged his dagger into Edmund's heart as the boy knelt begging and pleading for mercy. But this was not the only act of barbarity that Clifford would commit that day, and from this and his actions at the battle he earned the nickname 'The Boucher' (the butcher).

During the English Civil War the castle remained a Royalist stronghold and withstood a siege by the Parliamentarian forces that lasted for three long years. The garrison, which had been weakened by their deprivations, eventually surrendered in December 1645 and Oliver Cromwell gave orders for the roofs of the castle to be removed.

The last Clifford to own the castle was Lady Anne (1590–1676), and it was she who would make good the damage which the castle had suffered during the Civil War. Work began just three years after the end of the siege. To celebrate the completion of the repairs she planted a yew tree, which still stands in the centre of the castle's courtyard almost 500 years later.

Today Skipton Castle can proudly boast that it remains one of the best preserved mediaeval castles in England. Although the castle is open to the public, it contains a private residence and this part of the structure dates back to the time of Henry VIII.

BOLTON ABBEY

Arguably one of the dale's most famous landmarks must be the ruins of Bolton Priory, deep in the heart of Wharfedale. Originally the Augustinian priory was founded in 1120 at Embsay. The name Bolton Abbey refers to the estate on which the priory is located, and was established a number of years later, in 1151, by the monks. In 1154 the land, along with a number of other resources, was given to the order by Lady Alice de Romille of Skipton Castle. Scottish raiders in the early 14th century caused much damage to the fabric of the priory and for a short period the monks were forced to abandon the site. For many years the estate belonged to the Dukes of Devonshire and it is now owned by the Chatsworth Settlement Trustees, which was set up by Andrew Devonshire, the 11th Duke of Devonshire.

A well-known feature at Bolton Abbey is the notorious stretch of the River Wharfe called the Strid, where the water is forced into a deep and narrow channel. It is so called because it was once considered so narrow that one could stride across. Although it is only two metres wide at its narrowest point, and a very tempting prospect for the more adventurous, those who have failed in their attempts to leap the gap have landed in the water with tragic results, for there are no records of anyone ever surviving. Beneath this treacherous stretch of thundering water lie a number of caves and eroded tunnels, into which the victims are inevitably drawn and, unable to escape, are drowned. It is undeniably a beautiful place, but it is one which must be treated with the utmost respect and care, for the dangers which await the unwary and the foolhardy cannot be overestimated.

THE NORTH YORKSHIRE MOORS AND THE WOLDS

CROSSES AND STANDING STONES

In 1974 the North York Moors National Park adopted Young Ralph Cross as their emblem. The cross dates back to the 13th century and was originally made of wood. The present stone cross is thought to have been erected in the 18th century, when a Danby farmer named Ralph discovered the body of a penniless traveller who had died of exhaustion. Ralph decided to place the cross on the spot where he had found the unfortunate man.

In 1961 the cross collapsed when someone climbed it in search of coins, and was repaired by inserting a steel rod up through the shaft. Sadly, it has twice been vandalised, once by a vehicle using a tow rope to pull it down. Hopefully, it is now safe from these mindless acts of wilful destruction by pathetic individuals, for the cross has been relocated further back from the road.

Young Ralph Cross is one of many such crosses and monoliths, which can be found dotted over the moorland. As long as humans have inhabited the land these monuments have been erected. There are a number of reasons for their appearance; in some cases they were to mark the boundaries of ownership; some were memorials, in which case they could be true monuments to people such as Captain Cook (which can be found near Great Ayton), while others are simply crude stone markers which were erected to the memory of some humble soul; while other stones were erected as way markers to guide the traveller across the moors.

Another interesting cross which can be found standing on a disused pannier trod (a

Fat Betty.

The emblem of the North Yorkshire Moors: Young Ralph Cross.

stone pathway laid to facilitate the movement of ponies laden with goods across boggy land) not far from Young Ralph is the White Cross, which is perhaps better known as Fat Betty. There are a number of theories to how it got its name: one is that it was named after one of the nuns from Rosedale Abbey, called Sister Elizabeth. The Cistercian nuns were known as 'white ladies' because their gowns were made from undyed wool, and as the cross was painted white it is easy to see the connection. However, another story tells of a woman from Castleton, who was known as Fat Betty. One foggy night, while travelling home on the back of her husband's horse and cart, she lost her hold and fell. Her husband carried on, oblivious to the fact that his wife was missing. He only discovered her disappearance when he arrived home and, although he retraced his journey, all he ever found was a block of stone.

Once there were many more crosses than can be found today, but during the Reformation the cross was seen as idolatrous. On 28 August 1643 Parliament passed an Act which demanded that all monuments of superstition and idolatry must be destroyed. Many crosses were demolished, but fortunately a number did survive, albeit mostly as fragments of shafts and sockets.

These stones make up a valuable record of our heritage. Sadly, the inscriptions on many of them have not stood up to the ravages of time, and on those where the lettering may be still legible, often their meaning has long been forgotten. But even so they stand as monuments to our past and to the lives of our forefathers.

ROSEBERRY TOPPING

The area around Roseberry Topping has been inhabited for thousands of years and the distinctive hill has long drawn much attention. The Vikings regarded this hill as a special place and gave it the name Óðions bjarg (Odin's rock) which over time became corrupted to Roseberry: the word Topping is also derived from the Old Norse 'Toppen' meaning hill. The 10th-century English abbot Ælfric of Eynsham

Right: The Bridestones.

Far right: The distinctive shape of Roseberry Topping.

wrote that it was the practice among heathens to take offerings to Odin (or Wodan, the Germanic equivalent), which they brought to hill places.

In 1607 William Camden wrote of Roseberry Topping that it was a 'mighty height' and served as a landmark for sailors. He noted that there was a local rhyme, which says that 'when Roseberry wears a cap then Cleveland should beware a clap.' Camden also informs us that not only is the spring water which flows from the hill very beneficial for the curing of diseased eyes, but it has also caused the land below to be lush and fruitful.

In the 18th century the young James Cook developed his first taste for adventure while climbing on Roseberry Topping. The hill was once part of a large private estate and an old shooting box still remains at the base of the hill. On top of Roseberry Topping once stood a hermitage called Wilfred's Needle, which had been hewn out of the solid rock. Sadly this disappeared when quarrying work and mining for iron ore caused part of the summit to collapse at the beginning of the 20th century.

CAPTAIN COOK

Captain James Cook was born on 27 October 1728 in the village of East Marton, which is now located within the town boundaries of Middlesbrough. At an early age his family moved to Airey Holme Farm at Great Ayton. The local school where he was taught is now a museum and was first built in 1704 by Michael Postgate, and rebuilt in 1785. It had a small endowment with which to instruct eight poor children. James's studies were financed by his father's employee, Thomas Scottowe. At the age of 16 he left home to go to the fishing village of Staithes, where he was apprenticed to the local grocery-cum-haberdashery shop. Legend has it that it was while he was gazing through the shop window that he first felt the lure of the sea, and it was not long before the shop owner, William Sanderson, finding Cook unsuitable for the trade, took him to Whitby, where he introduced him to John and Henry Walker. This was to prove fortuitous for the young Cook as

A shooting box as seen from the top of Roseberry Topping.

The view from the summit of Roseberry Topping.

Right: The former schoolhouse at Great Ayton: James Cook was a pupil here.

Far right: A plaque on the side of the former schoolhouse commemorates its famous pupil.

the Walkers were prominent ship owners. They took him on as a merchant navy apprentice and his first assignment was on the collier *Freelove*. For the next few years he spent his time sailing between the Tyne and London on various coasters.

A monument to James Cook at Great Ayton.

Cook's apprenticeship lasted three years, during which time he learnt algebra, astronomy, geometry, navigation and trigonometry; all vital skills which he would need if he was ever to command his own ship. Once his apprenticeship had been completed he began working on trading ships in the Baltic. Cook rapidly worked his way through the ranks, starting as mate on the collier brig *Friendship*, where he was officer in charge of navigation. Three years later, in 1755, he was offered his own ship; however, a month later he volunteered for the Royal Navy. At the time Great Britain was rearming in preparation for what was to be the Seven Years' War, and Cook thought that there would be better opportunities for promotion. He would, though, be required to start on the bottom rung and on 17 June 1755 he boarded HMS *Eagle* as an able seaman. But again he was to achieve speedy promotion and he was soon the master's mate. Two years after joining the Royal Navy he passed his master's exam, which meant that he was qualified to handle and navigate a ship of the king's fleet.

It was during the Seven Years' War (a war described by Sir Winston Churchill as truly being the first World War, for it involved every major power of the time) that Cook's skills as a surveyor and cartographer were to be put to full use. He was tasked with mapping the entrance of the Saint Lawrence River during the siege, which allowed General Wolfe to make his famous attack on the Plains of Abraham. The battle left Quebec City in British hands, but both Wolfe and his French counterpart died from wounds received at the battle. This battle was also to be the turning point in Cook's career, for it brought him to the attention of both the Admiralty and the Royal Society, and led to him becoming commander of HM Bark *Endeavour* in 1766. The term 'Bark' refers to a vessel which is nondescript and does not fit into any of the navy's other categories. The *Endeavour* had started life as a collier and was bought by the navy to be converted to undertake exploration.

Cook was hired by the Royal Society to sail to the Pacific Ocean, where his mission was to

observe and document the transit of Venus across the sun. In 1768 the *Endeavour* sailed from England and Cook set her course around Cape Horn, arriving at Tahiti on 13 April 1769. It was from there that the observations were to be made, but these proved inconclusive. Cook later mapped the coastline of New Zealand, after which he sailed west, where he eventually reached the south-eastern coast of Australia on 19 April 1770. He was the first recorded European to have landed on the east coast and four days later he wrote about his first encounter with Australian aborigines, noting in his journal that he had seen a number of people who had appeared black in colour, but that he was not sure if that was their true colour or if they were wearing something. Perhaps we can draw the conclusion from this that his first encounter with them was not a particularly close one. He eventually returned to England, arriving home on 12 July 1771.

In 1775 he was promoted to Captain and by now his fame had extended far beyond the Admiralty. He was made a Fellow of the Royal Society and awarded the Copley Gold Medal (which is awarded for distinguished achievement in any field of science). His portrait was painted by the notable English painter, Sir Nathaniel Dance-Holland, and it now hangs in the National Maritime Museum in Greenwich. The House of Lords described him as 'the first navigator of Europe' and he was even to dine with Dr Johnson's famous biographer, James Boswell. The lure of the sea, however, proved too strong for Cook and in 1776 he set out on his third and final voyage, which was to end with tragic consequences. He was to command HMS *Resolution*, the same ship that he had commanded on his second voyage, and his mission was to attempt to discover the Northwest Passage. In 1778 he became the first European to visit the Hawaiian Islands, which he named the Sandwich Islands, after the fourth Earl of Sandwich, who was First

The famous Cook monument at Whitby.

Lord of the Admiralty. He then sailed on, travelling north-east, where he was to chart much of the North American north-west coastline. But this was a troubled voyage and Cook developed a stomach ailment, which is thought to have led to him behaving erratically and being quarrelsome. This was a different Cook to the man whom the sailors had known and respected previously; the even-tempered and well-liked leader had vanished and was replaced by a man given to fits of temper.

He returned to Hawaii the following year, where he stayed for a month. However, shortly after setting sail, the foremast of the *Resolution* broke, forcing him to return to the islands. It is not known for certain why on this return he was made so unwelcome by the Hawaiians, but it is thought that it may have coincided with the ending of a series of festivals dedicated to the Polynesian god Lono, or perhaps he had simply outstayed his welcome. Whatever the cause, there was tension between the Hawaiians and the Europeans and a number of quarrels broke out. On 14 February 1779 a number of Hawaiians stole one of the small boats belonging to Cook. Theft was quite common among the islands and Cook would normally take hostages until the stolen goods were returned. On this occasion he attempted to take the Chief of Hawaii as his hostage. The

islanders, however, prevented this and Cook and his men were forced to retreat to the beach. While attempting to help launch the boats, Cook was struck on the head and as he fell face forward he was stabbed to death and his body was dragged away. Four of the mariners who accompanied him were also killed and two were wounded.

During the 12 years that Captain James Cook sailed around the Pacific Ocean he contributed much to Europe's knowledge of the area and unquestionably his legacy consisted of his achievements in the field of navigation. The respect for this great captain and navigator was such that Benjamin Franklin wrote to the captains of the American warships (in 1779 Britain was still at war with America in the War of Independence) that if they should come upon Cook's vessel they should 'not consider her an enemy, nor suffer any plunder to be made of the effects contained in her, nor obstruct her immediate return to England by detaining her or sending her into any other part of Europe or to America; but that you treat the said Captain Cook and his people with all civility and kindness…as common friends to mankind'. Franklin's words spoke volumes about the respect and admiration which was universally felt for this great sailor, who as a youth dreamed of adventures at sea while an apprentice to a shopkeeper at Staithes, and whose name is still revered today.

WHARRAM PERCY

It is currently estimated that there are about 3,000 deserted villages in England. The most common reason for their abandonment was the Black Death plague which struck England in 1348, during which a settlement's population was often so reduced that it proved impossible for it to continue. This, however, was not the cause of the demise of Wharram Percy, which is perhaps England's most famous deserted village. Not only did it survive this

The ruinous St Martin's Church at Wharram Percy.

The outline of the foundations of a house at Wharram Percy.

great scourge, but it also existed for at least another 100 years.

It was another human affliction which spelled the end for this settlement – that of pure greed. Documentary evidence dating back to 1517 reveals that it was the local lord of the manor, Baron Hilton, who, keen to make financial gain, evicted the families from their homes and demolished the buildings. The woollen industry was growing, and there was more profit to be made from sheep rearing than arable farming. The baron simply wanted the land to increase the size of his flock.

Today all that remains of the village is the ruinous St Martin's Church. The houses, like the villagers, have long gone; though archaeological excavations have unearthed the outlines of some of their foundations. These have revealed that the village consisted of longhouses, which were not only the homes of the village folk, but also of their cattle.

It is thought that the roots of the settlement can be traced back to well before the Roman conquest of Britain; however, for many centuries Wharram Percy was little more than a

hamlet. It did not reach village status until the time of the Normans, and it reached its peak sometime in the late 13th century, when it is thought that it may have had a population of between 150 and 180 people.

The church of St Martin's was still being regularly used as late as 1870, by which time a new church had been built in the neighbouring village of Thixendale. But it was not until 1949 that it began to fall into decay, for in that year the lead from the roof was stolen and this allowed water to seep into the fabric of the building. In 1959 further damage was caused when a storm resulted in part of the tower collapsing. Although it now stands as a ruin, many parts of the building are remarkably well preserved, and once a year a service is still performed within its walls.

KIRKHAM PRIORY

The ancient ruins of Kirkham Priory were to play a significant role in recent historic events, as the area was used to test landing craft prior to the D-Day landings in Normandy during World War Two. Two months prior to the

The bridge at Kirkham, which spans the River Derwent.

invasion the site was secretly visited by an exhausted Winston Churchill, who had travelled through the night by train to inspect the troops as they trained and give them words of encouragement. During his visit he was given a demonstration of an amphibious lorry swimming through water.

The Augustinian priory had been founded by the Lord of Helmsley, Walter l'Espec, in the 1120s, on the banks of the River Derwent. According to legend, he built it in memory of his only son, who was killed when he was flung from his horse while out riding on land nearby. It is uncertain why the young teenager was unseated

The ruins of Kirkham Priory gatehouse.

from his mount. Some say that his horse was startled by a wild boar, while other accounts say that he was a wild youth who had simply been thrown while racing.

Little is known about the priory's history; however, excavations have revealed that it was intended to be a lavish place of worship. We do know that shortly after its foundation it was faced with closure, as there was a growing popularity for Cistercian communities, and it appears that there may have been an attempt to resite those monks wishing to remain in the Augustinian order. The idea was to bring Kirkham under Cistercian rule, and some form of agreement had been reached with the Cistercian community at Rievaulx Abbey, but nothing more is known of this, other than that Kirkham Priory continued to be a holy house until the Dissolution in 1539.

RIEVAULX ABBEY

Rievaulx Abbey was founded by St Bernard of Clairvaux in 1132, and it was the first Cistercian monastery to be established in the north of England. St Bernard had sent a group of monks, led by his secretary William, from his abbey at Clairvaux to establish the order in Yorkshire. Regarded as one of the greatest figures in the Middle Ages, St Bernard was instrumental in the development of the Cistercian Order. Born in 1090 at Fontaine in Burgundy, he joined the community at Cîteaux when he was about 22 years old. He arrived there at a crucial point in the history of the order, and he is described by many as being the second founder of the Cistercians. His charisma and energy was such that within three years of his arrival the abbot of Cîteaux, Stephen Harding, sent him to establish Clairvaux (valley of light).

St Bernard's magnetism was so great that it is said that wives would conceal their husbands and mothers their sons for fear that they might be drawn to the order. One of his critics wrote scathingly that St Bernard would send carts into the town to fill with recruits. One of those who answered his call was the future Pope Eugenius III. Although St Bernard would actively reject publicity, he played a prominent part in contemporary affairs. As well as establishing over 350 religious houses, he also left a considerable body of writings, which includes sermons, mystical works and over 300 letters. He strongly believed that one discovered God through prayer and devotion, and not through the 'idle curiosity' of books.

The abbey of Rievaulx would attract many powerful benefactors, including Henry II (1133–1189) and David I of Scotland (1080–1154). In time the abbey would become one of the wealthiest in England, with a community of 140 monks and many more lay brothers. The monks built up very profitable businesses mining both iron and lead, and rearing sheep to sell the wool. Their fortunes would peak during the mid-12th century, especially under Abbot Aelred, who held the office from 1147 to 1167. He had been the former steward of David I and had entered Rievaulx as a monk in 1134. He proved to be a dynamic leader and the abbey flourished under his guidance. Aelred was a prominent figure, who became known by many as 'Bernard of the North'.

By the end of the 13th century, however, Rievaulx was facing a serious financial crisis. It had overextended itself with a number of building projects and had created a large debt. An outbreak of the highly contagious sheep-scab had meant that they were unable to sell wool. On top of this, the population had been severely reduced by the Black Death in 1348, which had made it difficult for them to recruit lay brothers needed for manual labour. The outcome of these problems was that by 1381 the community had been dramatically reduced to 14 monks, three lay brothers and the abbot.

By the time the abbey was dissolved in 1538 there had been a slight increase in numbers, but nothing like the strength that the community had had at its height. At the time of its closure the monks had built a prototype blast furnace at Laskill, which is thought to have been as efficient as a modern one. They were able to produce cast iron of a very good quality, and it has been said that had the monks been allowed to continue with their work, we might have entered the industrial age a good two and a half centuries earlier.

After the abbey was closed, Henry VIII ordered that all the valuables should be removed and the buildings rendered uninhabitable. The estates were sold to the Earl of Rutland at a very favourable price. In the late 17th century it passed into the Duncombe family, and in the 1750s Thomas Duncombe created a terrace with two Grecian-style temples in the grounds. Today Rievaulx Abbey is cared for by English Heritage.

HELMSLEY CASTLE

The ancient market town of Helmsley predates the Norman Conquest of 1066, and is recorded in the *Domesday Book* as Elmeslac. After the conquest, William granted the estate to his half-brother Robert de Mortain. However, in 1088 William Rufus confiscated it. It is not known for certain whether Robert had built a castle here, but records show that the castle, which now dominates the town's skyline, was definitely in existence by 1120, when it was owned by Walter l'Espec. It is thought that he may have built it merely to mark out the centre of his estate, as the stronghold's position has little strategic merit.

Walter, as well as being a soldier, was also a justiciar (the chief political and legal officer to the royal court) and as such he would be called upon to deputise for the king in his absence. In 1138 he fought against the Scots at the Battle of the Standard. When he died in 1154, having no children to leave his estate to, he granted much of his lands to Rievaulx Abbey, and the castle passed to his sister Adelina, who was married to Peter de Roos. Their son, Robert de Roos, began to replace

the old wooden castle with a stone structure in 1186, and instead of building the usual single keep he constructed two main towers, complete with two additional round-corner towers.

The castle remained the property of the de Roos family until 1478, when it was sold by Edmund de Roos to Richard, Duke of Gloucester, the most powerful man in Yorkshire, who later would become Richard III. The picture which has been portrayed of the man, of a monster with a withered arm and a humpback, was first written about by Sir Thomas More in his celebrated history. He also attributed all manner of crimes to the dead king, some of which were almost certainly impossible for him to have committed. More described Richard as evil incarnate, while Henry Tudor was the saviour, all sweetness and innocence, who slew the beast at Bosworth and freed the people of England from an accursed tyrant. This image was later reinforced by Shakespeare in his play *Richard III*. However, although the real man was undoubtedly not a saint, he has been much maligned. Interestingly, Sir Thomas More obtained his information directly from the Tudor king and therefore we

Helmsley Castle.

can suspect that his description may contain more than a little exaggeration. As to Richard's terrible and disfiguring deformities, More is the first to make note of them, for it appears no other in the lifetime of the fallen king makes mention of these. We must, therefore, conclude that this character assassination was simply a propaganda exercise designed to sully the former dynasty and praise the new régime.

After the death of Richard the castle was restored to Edmund de Roos by Henry VII. In 1508 Edmund died without an heir, so his property passed to his cousin, Sir George Manners of Etal. He died five years later, leaving the castle to his son Thomas, who was created Earl of Rutland in 1525 in recognition for his loyalty to the Crown. In 1533 Thomas had the abbot of Rievaulx Abbey removed and replaced with one who was more sympathetic to the Protestant cause. As a reward for this he was able, after the Dissolution, to purchase the estates of Rievaulx for a mere pittance.

During the Civil War Helmsley Castle, like many others in Yorkshire, was a Royalist stronghold. It was, therefore, a prime target for the Parliamentarian forces, which laid siege to it in September 1644. The besieged garrison only managed to hold out until November, when it was forced to surrender as food supplies ran out. As with many of the other castles in Yorkshire, once it was in Parliamentarian hands much of it was destroyed to prevent further use.

In 1688 the castle was sold to Charles Duncombe (1648–1711), a banker and politician, who in 1708 became the Lord Mayor of London. Duncombe started his working life as an apprentice goldsmith, and would later be admitted to the Worshipful Company of Goldsmiths. But it was in banking which he would make his fortune, and by the time of his death in 1711 he was the richest commoner in England. In 1685 he was elected to Parliament as a Tory, and during this period he opposed the establishment of the Bank of England. In 1688,

when James II fled the country, he asked Duncombe for a loan of £1,500, but this was refused.

After buying Helmsley Castle, Duncombe created a new mansion house on land located near to the town and called it Duncombe Park. The grounds were set out with great elegance and taste, and those adjoining the house were terraced so as to afford magnificent views, but it was not until 1713 that the house was totally completed.

In 1698 Duncombe was arrested for tax fraud and imprisoned in the Tower of London, which led to him being expelled from the House of Commons. Subsequently he was acquitted when it was discovered that the information had been incorrect, and on 20 October 1699 he was knighted. On his death in 1711 his brother-in-law and business partner Thomas Brown inherited the castle and estate. Thomas changed his name to Duncombe and lived in the mansion house, and it was he who finally completed the house. Today, this great house and magnificent grounds, as well the castle which is cared for by English Heritage, are still owned by the family, and are open to the public.

APPLETON-LE-MOORS

First mentioned in the *Domesday Book*, the charming ancient village of Appleton-le-Moors still retains its mediaeval layout. Evidence of early inhabitants has been unearthed, including their flint tools and Roman coins. The village possesses a particularly fine example of a 19th-century church, which has earned the well-deserved description of being 'the little gem of moorland churches'. It was designed by the architect J.L. Pearson, who would later build the magnificent cathedral in Truro, Cornwall. The church cost £10,000 to construct, and was paid for by Mary Shepherd, the widow of John Shepherd (1804–1862).

John had been born in the village and had started life in humble circumstances. He left to go to sea, where he made his fortune as a whaler

Right: Christ Church at Appleton-le-Moors: this church was described by John Betjeman as 'a little gem among moorland churches.'

Far right: The shaft of a 10th or 11th-century stone cross outside the Church of St Gregory in the village of Cropton.

Far right: This well in the village of Cropton was once 300 feet deep, but was capped in about 1920. It used two buckets on an endless rope and as one bucket came up full the other one went down empty.

and eventually became a ship owner. In the 1850s he returned to Appleton-le-Moors, now a wealthy man and determined to help his native village. He was particularly keen to provide an education for the children, for it was an opportunity which he had never had. Unfortunately, he died before he could see his plans fulfilled. His widow, however, made sure that his wishes were carried out, and as well as the church she built the village school.

Along the main street stands a cottage with three faces carved in stone. It is said that they represent a lawyer, a doctor and a clergyman, and they are called the Three Bloodsuckers.

The Three Bloodsuckers!

Whoever they were it is obvious that with their uncharitable names they must not have been held in high esteem by the village folk of Appleton-le-Moors.

RYEDALE FOLK MUSEUM

In the village of Hutton-le-Hole is located the excellent Ryedale Folk Museum, which takes the visitor upon an exciting journey through the history of Ryedale. The site covers three acres and has numerous exhibits, including an Iron Age settlement, a manor house and an original Edwardian photographic studio, complete with a mahogany camera, which once belonged to the portrait photographer William Hayes, who

Earthworks of the Roman military complex at Cawthorn.

Far left: An Edwardian photographic studio.

Left: A journey back in time at the Ryedale Folk Museum – a shop from the 1950s.

Left: A witch-post. It is believed that these protected the dwelling from witches.

had set up business in 1902 in York. The studio was moved to the Ryedale Folk Museum in the late 1980s and has been captivating visitors ever since. There is even a village shop which transports the visitor back to the early 1950s. The museum is an exciting microcosm of Yorkshire as it once was, and an experience which should not be missed.

Far left: Hutton-le-Hole.

One of the fabulous Anglo-Saxon and Viking carved stones in the church of St Oswald's: this broken stone displays the legs of two wrestling men.

ST OSWALD'S AT LYTHE

There has been a church at Lythe since about 900, when the first church would have been made of wood. At the time the parish of Lythe extended over 40 square miles and included villages such as Egton and Ugthorpe: the parish has now been greatly reduced. The name Lythe means 'on a hill', which is very apt as, due to its high vantage point, the church offers stunning views of the coast.

With the arrival of the Normans the wooden church was replaced with a more substantial stone building. There is no mention of the church in the *Domesday Book*, but it is recorded that there was a Manor of Lythe, which was held by one Nigel, and as we already know there was a church located here, it is fair to assume that this was merely an oversight by the compilers. In 1100 Nigel's son, Robert Fossard, made a grant of the church to Nostell Priory (near Wakefield). After the Dissolution the church was granted to the Bygods. However, after the execution of Sir Francis Bygod on 2 June 1537

Far right: This is a 'hogback' gravestone and depicts a man with his arms in the mouths of wild beasts. It is thought that it may be a representation of Ragnarök, which translated means 'the final destiny of the gods' or 'the twilight of the gods' and in Norse legend spells the end of the world.

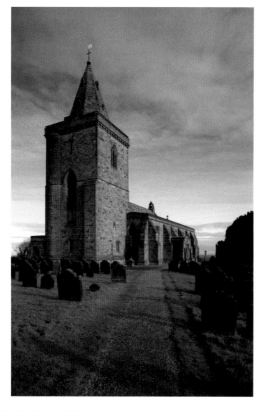

St Oswald's at Lythe.

for his part in the Pilgrimage of Grace, the church reverted to Henry VIII, who gave it to the Archbishop of York.

Although the original stone church would have been built in the Early English style, this is difficult to distinguish, since the building has been altered and rebuilt on a number of occasions. The present church owes more to Sir Walter Tapper and his restoration of 1910. In 1768 the top of the steeple was removed when it was feared that it could fall on to the church, and a year later the whole building was taken down to its foundations and rebuilt. The church does, however, retain a number of interesting early features, such as the mediaeval *piscinae* which can be found in the south wall of the chancel.

However, perhaps the church's greatest treasure is the collection of Anglo-Saxon and Viking carvings. Discovered during the restoration of 1910, these magnificent carved stones date mainly from the 10th century. Most of the stones are funeral monuments, which come from a Christian graveyard and consist of 'hogback' gravestones, incised slabs, cross-heads and shafts. This exciting find has turned out to be one of the largest and most important collections of its type in the country.

HOLE OF HORCUM

According to tradition, the geographical feature of the Hole of Horcum was formed during an argument between the giant Wade and his wife, Bell. The giant flew into a rage and scooped up a handful of earth, which he flung at his wife and in doing so created the Hole of Horcum. She deftly avoided the oncoming projectile and where it landed a hill, which is called Blackey Topping, was formed.

In reality, this magnificent 400-foot deep natural amphitheatre, although it may appear manmade, was formed many thousands of years ago by the action of water erosion.

Wade was also credited with creating the Roman road on Wheeldale Moor near Goathland. The road is known as Wade's Causeway and it is said that he built it so that his wife could drive her cows over the boggy moor.

HINDERWELL

In the grounds of St Hilda's Church stands a well of spring water. According to legend, the founder of Whitby Abbey, St Hilda, would stop here to refresh herself while journeying through the district. Another version informs us that she had a cell here, to which she would occasionally retire to meditate. Whichever version is true, it is certainly the village's connection to St Hilda that gives it its name, which is a corruption of Hildreuuelle (Hilder's Well).

The Hole of Horcum.

St Hilda's at Hinderwell.

St Hilda's Well.

In 1603 a plague broke out in the village, killing a number of its inhabitants. The outbreak was traced back to a Turkish ship which had been stranded on the coast. Strangely, Hinderwell was the only settlement in the area to be affected.

GOATHLAND

The history of Goathland dates back to the times of the Vikings. Its name is derived from Anglo-Saxon and means 'Good Land' or 'God's Land'. The earliest written records for the settlement date back to 1100, when it was referred to as Godeland. In 1926 it changed its name to Goathland.

In 1267 the village and much of the surrounding area was given to Edmund Crouchback, 1st Earl of Lancaster, by his father Henry III. Four years later, Edmund was to accompany his elder brother, Edward, on the Ninth Crusade to Palestine. It is said that while there he earned his nickname 'Crouchback' (which is thought to mean 'cross back' and refers to his right to wear a cross on his back as a crusader). He had been created Earl of Lancaster in 1265.

In 1351 Henry of Grosmont, 3rd Earl of Lancaster, was made Duke of Lancaster and his land became a duchy. After his death the dukedom was transferred by charter to his son-in-law John of Gaunt, and was to pass to his legitimate male heirs in perpetuity. Today, Goathland still belongs to the duchy of Lancaster.

Goathland.

Left: A pinfold on the outskirts of Goathland, where stray animals were kept until their owners came forth to claim them and paid a fine for their release.

routes. On 26 May 1836 the line was opened. This meant that the village was now more accessible to those wishing to visit this delightful place. Goathland had already got a fledgling tourist industry, as people were attracted by the stunning scenery and clean air. With the coming of the railway, tourism would flourish.

For hundreds of years there has been a common grazing right on the village green and surrounding moorland, so it is quite usual to see sheep casually wandering along the streets of the village. On the outskirts of Goathland stands a stone pinfold, which was used to impound stray animals until a fine had been paid by their owner. There is one animal which

Far left: An unusual gravestone in the churchyard at Goathland. The anchor marks the grave of a master mariner and his wife.

At the beginning of the 1830s it was decided that a railway should be built, which would go through the village. In 1832 the famous engineer George Stephenson (9 June 1781–12 August 1848), also known as the 'Father of Railways', was asked to produce a report on a number of possible

Left: A pannier trod at Goathland.

Far left: The war memorial at Goathland is a replica of the seventh-century Lilla Cross. The original cross can be found on Fylingdales Moor.

The level crossing at Grosmont.

This is thought to be the world's earliest passenger railway tunnel. It was built between 1833 and 1835 by George Stephenson and the first carriages to run through it were horse-drawn.

one would not wish to meet and that is the dreadful gytrash (or padfoot). It is said that this fearsome beast wanders the countryside around Goathland. The gytrash takes the shape of an enormous black goat, with burning eyes like red-hot coals and horns tipped with flames. The legend dates back to pagan times, when a local lord built himself a castle. To protect himself from his enemies, he walled up a local maiden called Gytha into the foundation of his fortress. But he was to spend the rest of his days racked with guilt at his evil deed and on the night that he died this terrible gytrash first appeared.

Many say that the beast is the ghost of this wicked lord, whose restless spirit is doomed to wander the land, filling the local folk with terror. It is, however, unlikely that you will meet this hellish beast today, for it is said that a local witch (a white one presumably) drove this apparition away by casting a spell.

Today, the village of Goathland is famous for being the location of the popular television series *Heartbeat*.

THE VENERABLE NICHOLAS POSTGATE

Nicholas Postgate was born in about 1597 at Kirkdale House in Egton Bridge. It appears that he was a typical youth, with a happy-go-lucky nature. Even at an early age, however, he possessed a strong conviction about his Catholic faith. These were dangerous times for Catholics in England. In 1585 Elizabeth I passed a law (Act against Jesuits and Seminarists) that was infamous for being the harshest among the many penal laws and one which dictated that a Catholic priest could be condemned to death for treason: to be hung, drawn and quartered.

In protest at the suppression of his faith, Nicholas joined a group of travelling players, who mocked the authorities with verse, song and dance. In January 1616 he was fined 10 shillings at Helmsley Quarter Sessions for his activities. At the sessions he was described as a 13-year-old labourer from Egton (however, this was clearly an error, as he would have been 19 at the time).

In 1621 he travelled to France, where he joined the English College at Douai. While at the college he used the alias Whitmore; it was common among students to adopt a false name so as to protect the identity of their families at home. Nicholas was later to use his mother's maiden name of Watson.

After being ordained as a priest on 20 March 1628, it was time for him to consider returning to England to begin his work. Therefore, in 1630, fully aware of the dangers he faced, Nicholas sailed for England. On 29 June 1630 he landed at Whitby and, setting off on foot, he made his way to Saxton Hall, near Tadcaster, to take up his first employment. It was here that he was to become chaplain to Lady Hungate. Many of the gentry secretly remained Catholics, but for appearances' sake would attend Church of England services. Failure to conform to this new state religion could incur heavy penalties; from hefty fines to people even losing their estates. Many of the large country houses had hiding places called 'priest-holes' built into them and also secret chapels where they could worship. It was far too dangerous to openly employ a priest; many, therefore, would be taken on under the guise of a gardener. Although it is difficult to know for sure under what guise Postgate would have been employed by Lady Hungate, a document which can be found in the Bodleian Library refers to Sir William Hungate's butler as being called Nicholas.

Father Postgate's long vocation as a Catholic priest took him all over Yorkshire, including Bradford, Halifax, Hull, Ripon and Richmond, until in the 1660s he finally settled at Ugthorpe.

It was here that for the next 20 years he walked the moors and Eskdale. He set up home in a humble house, which is now known as the Hermitage of Ugthorpe. He was a man of simple faith, who was renowned for his humanity and care of the poor. Father Postgate was a holy man, who was a friend of both Catholics and Protestants alike.

As the 17th century progressed, much of the anti-Catholic feeling began to die down, although Catholics still needed to be somewhat vigilant as there remained some risk from the authorities. In 1678, however, a popish plot was uncovered by Titus Oates. This plot, which entailed the killing of Charles II and his replacement by his Catholic brother, James, was a total fabrication and the product of Oates's warped and fertile mind. But it had the desired effect of stirring up old hatreds. According to Oates, he had discovered this heinous plot when he had infiltrated a group of Jesuits. He furthered fanned the flames by stating that they planned to murder thousands of Protestants.

Sir Edmund Berry Godfrey, a prominent Protestant magistrate in London, was murdered and Oates, quick to capitalise on the crime, soon laid the blame on the Catholics. John Reeves, who had been the manservant of Sir Edmund, vowed that he would take revenge. He set out for Whitby, possibly because the port was a well-known landing point for Catholic priests. While there he discovered that Father Postgate was to baptise a child at nearby Ugglebarnby. With the help of a certain William Cockerill, he raided the place where the ceremony was being held during the baptism. They took the elderly priest to Brompton (near Scarborough), where he was brought in front of the local magistrate, Sir William Cayley. The magistrate, after hearing the evidence from Reeves and a number of witnesses, sent Father Postgate to York to stand trial. It is said that Reeves was to receive a reward for his information, which was believed to be 30 pieces of silver. Perhaps it was the fact that he later

Right: The Roman Catholic Church of St Hedda in Egton Bridge, which contains relics of the martyr Nicholas Postgate.

Far right: Annunciation – one of the Stations of the Cross. This tablet is on the side of the church of St Hedda's.

committed suicide in Littlebeck, near Sleights, which encouraged a number of folk to make comparisons between Reeves and Judas Iscariot.

While incarcerated in York Castle, Father Postgate wrote a hymn, which is still sung at Egton Bridge and in the surrounding district. When the trial began it soon was to turn into a farce, as the judge wanted to acquit the old man, but the jury insisted that he was guilty. Therefore, on 7 August 1679, at the grand age of 82, Father Postgate was strapped to a wooden sledge and dragged from Micklegate Bar to Knavesmire, where he was hung, drawn and quartered. His quarters were given to his friends to bury and one of his hands was sent to the college at Douai. The crucifix which had been around his neck is now kept at Ampleforth Abbey.

LASTINGHAM

In 654 a monastery was built at Lastingham. The site had been given to St Cedd by Æthelwald, the under-king of Deira. Cedd was a bishop among the East Saxons of Essex, but he had often travelled north to Northumbria. It

was during these visits that he became intimate with Æthelwald, who would turn to the wise priest to administer the Word and the sacraments of the faith. During the period of

Far right: St Cedd's Well.

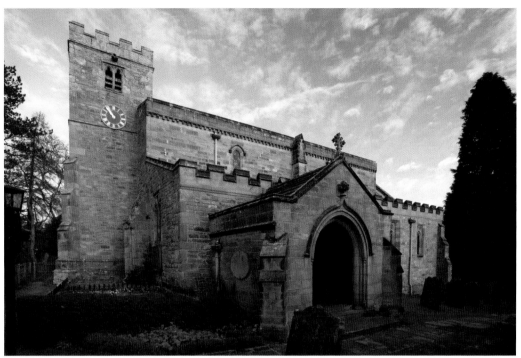

St Mary's Church in Lastingham.

Lent Cedd fasted, surviving on a little bread, one hen's egg and a drop of milk mixed with water. By this ritual fast and prayer he purified the site before the monastery could be built.

In 664 Cedd succumbed to the plague and his body was buried at Lastingham, rather than among his kinfolk in Essex. The nearness of the monastery to the coast (Lastingham being a few miles inland from Whitby) meant that it was susceptible to Viking raids and eventually it was abandoned and allowed to fall into ruin. In 1078 Stephen, the Abbot of Whitby, was granted permission to rebuild the monastery. Initially a crypt was built as a shrine to St Cedd, on the spot where it is thought he was buried. Work was then begun on the rest of the monastery, but was abandoned in 1088 when Stephen moved to York.

In 1228 the site became a parochial church and the unfinished abbey was used as the basis for the present church. Over the following centuries the building underwent many

Far left: The steps to the fantastic crypt in St Mary's. Walking in the crypt one is following in the footsteps of saints.

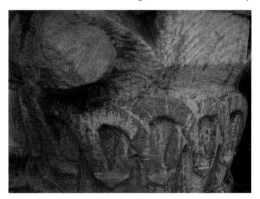

Left: Anglo-Saxon carving in the crypt.

The Blacksmith's Arms.

Opposite:

Top: Rosedale.

Bottom: The remains of a pair of kilns at Bank Top, Rosedale, which in former days would have been used to remove the impurities from the ironstone.

alterations and additions. The crypt, which remains and is easily accessible to the visitor, is an unforgettable experience, for as one enters this holy place a feeling of utmost peace and serenity fills one's heart. A sign in the porch of the church tells the visitor that when they step into the crypt they are following in the footsteps of saints. It is an experience not to be missed.

In the village of Lastingham there are three holy wells, which are dedicated to St Cedd, St Chad and St Ovin. In former times these wells would have been part of the village's water supply.

As with many communities, a public house can be found near the church and Lastingham is no exception, for opposite the church stands the Blacksmith's Arms. In the 18th century this was run by the vicar's wife. The vicar's annual stipend was only £20, and with 13 children to feed it was necessary for the family to have a second source of income. The Reverend Jeremiah Carter, however, was to fall foul of the ecclesiastical authorities for playing the fiddle in the pub between Sunday services. When brought before them he stated in his defence that dancing protected the youths from the evils of drinking too much, for while they were dancing they could not be drinking. It appears that this was acceptable as a valid argument and the vicar was acquitted.

ROSEDALE ABBEY

The village of Rosedale Abbey is renowned for its views, located as it is in the dramatic valley at the centre of Rosedale. It once was the site of a Cistercian priory, which sadly has all but disappeared, apart from a sundial, a single pillar and a staircase. The priory was originally founded in 1158 and was home to a small community of nuns. It is said that the nuns were the first people in the region to farm sheep commercially. The priory became yet another victim of the Dissolution of the Monasteries and was closed in 1535. Over the centuries, the stonework was plundered for use on local building projects, which included a new church that was built on the site of the former priory.

BEGGAR'S BRIDGE

This packhorse bridge which crosses the River Esk was built in 1619 by Thomas Ferris. As a young man, he had courted Agnes Richardson, who was the daughter of the local squire.

Beggar's Bridge.

Thomas came from humble origins and was not considered suitable for the hand of Agnes. He therefore decided to go to sea to make his fortune. On the evening before he was due to sail he had arranged to meet her to bid her farewell, but it was not to be, for he was unable to cross the River Esk as it was in full flood. So he left for sea without saying goodbye. In time he made his fortune and returned to marry his sweetheart. He constructed the bridge so that no one else would have to encounter the same problem.

PICKERING

According to legend, Pickering was founded in 270BC by Peredurus, King of the Brigantes. While fishing in a nearby river, he had lost his ring, which was recovered sometime later from the stomach of a pike: PIKE – RING. There are a number of versions of this tale and whether there is any truth to this legend we shall never know. However, a pike with a ring in its mouth features on the town's coat of arms.

After the Norman Conquest, William the Conqueror commanded that a castle was to be built at Pickering. Initially it was a motte and

The Church of St Peter and St Paul in Pickering.

bailey fortress made from timber, which was later replaced by a much stronger stone construction. To the north of Pickering is a forest that was used by royalty for hunting deer and wild boar. During the castle's history it was

visited by a number of monarchs: Henry II stayed here with his mistress 'the fair Rosamund', and King John played backgammon in the castle's Great Hall.

During the Middle Ages it was not uncommon for the interiors of churches to be highly decorated, including detailed wall paintings. Sadly, during the Reformation many of these colourful decorations and paintings were removed, and churches became much plainer and more sombre places, as befitting the puritanical outlook of the time. Although many of these wonderful wall paintings were destroyed, a number thankfully survived. The parish church of St Peter and St Paul's in Pickering is one example where these remarkable decorations managed to escape destruction. In the 15th century the paintings were covered by lime-wash, which has protected them for future generations. They were to remain forgotten until in the mid-19th century they were uncovered during work on the interior. Once uncovered, they created a great stir and crowds flocked to the church to

marvel at the forgotten treasures. Three weeks later Reverend Ponsonby had them covered over again, and so they remained for the next quarter of a century, until Reverend Lightfoot decided that they should be uncovered and restored.

A delightful stone font.

Pickering Castle.

Standing looking at the fabulous paintings, it is not difficult to imagine the effect they would have had on the mediaeval worshippers, and especially powerful must have been the image of 'the descent into Hell'. What fear and dread must have been instilled into them by this graphic image, and how clear the message of what would befall them if they were to stray from the path of the good Christian – a dire warning for those tempted to sin.

ST GREGORY'S MINSTER

It is thought that a church has stood on this site since 645. We know that the original church was destroyed by marauding Vikings and that it was rebuilt in 1055. We also know that it was rebuilt by Orm Gamelson, for a remarkable sundial with Old English inscriptions tells us this fact. The sundial is the best surviving example of a stone inscription from Saxon times and owes its excellent preservation to it having been covered with plaster for many centuries. It was during building work carried out in 1771 that this amazing sundial, which spans seven feet, was revealed above the main door. Since then, it has been further protected from the elements as a stone porch was erected.

This delightful late-Saxon church has a number of exciting features to interest the visitor. A number of Saxon crosses and intricately carved stones have been used in the outside walls, and no doubt have been rescued from the previous building.

St Gregory's Minster.

Far Right: The ancient sundial above the main door of St Gregory's.

Left: Anglo-Saxon crosses and carvings which have been incorporated into the walls of St Gregory's.

THORNTON-LE-DALE

The pretty picture postcard village of Thornton-le-Dale has a history which dates back across the millennia into prehistoric times. Exotic animals such as mammoths, hyenas and rhinoceroses once roamed freely across this land and their remains have been unearthed, but these creatures migrated south to warmer climes with the arrival of the Ice Age. Evidence of early man can be found in the parish of Thornton in the shape of 14 tumuli, while stone and flint weapons have also been discovered.

In time, the warlike Celtic tribe of the Brigantes invaded the district, and ruled the land until they in turn were subjugated by the Romans, who invaded Britain in AD43 under Emperor Claudius. The Brigantes were either massacred or forced to yield to the new authority. After the Romans deserted Britain, the Anglo-Saxon raiders took advantage of their absence and began to conquer the area in about 500. The name Thornton is derived from Anglo-Saxon and suggests that the area may have been thickly wooded with thorn trees.

Perhaps one of the most photographed cottages in Yorkshire, this beautiful thatched cottage in its picture postcard setting can be found in the village of Thornton-le-Dale.

179

The main road leading into Thornton-le-Dale.

Originally, it was simply called Thornton, but with the arrival of the railways 'Dale' was added to the name so as to distinguish it from the other Thorntons in the region. In the early 20th century 'le' was added as it was considered to sound upmarket and more befitting a village which is still described as the most beautiful in Yorkshire.

BROMPTON-BY-SAWDON

On the road between Scarborough and Pickering lies the quaint village of Brompton-by-Sawdon. It possesses one of the finest village churches in Yorkshire, in which on 4 October 1802 William Wordsworth married Mary Hutchinson. The ceremony was presided over by John Ellis and witnessed by Thomas, John and Joanna Hutchinson.

It is thought that the village was once the residence of the kings of Northumbria, and a mound called Castle Hill may attest to this, for the name suggests that some form of fortification or stronghold stood here. It is further thought, however, that it may have been a motte and bailey construction from Norman times.

THE FATHER OF BRITISH AERONAUTICS

Sir George Cayley put the question of manned flight into a nutshell when he stated, 'The whole problem is confined within these limits, viz: to make a surface support a given weight by the

The stained-glass window in All Saints' church in Brompton-by-Sawdon depicts the story of the village.

Interior of the delightful All Saints' church in Brampton-by-Sawdon.

application of power to the resistance of the air.' Born in 1773, 130 years before the Wright brothers were to enter the record books for their first controlled and powered flight, Sir George was to become a pioneer of aviation. It is fair to say that the brothers would owe their eventual success to his early work.

He built his first flying machine in 1796 at the age of 23: a model helicopter. Eight years later he designed and constructed a model monoplane glider, which had a surprisingly modern appearance. There is no doubt that in many ways Sir George was a man ahead of his time. He had inherited Brompton Hall and sufficient wealth from his father, which meant that he could concentrate on his lifelong passion for aeronautics. Every young man of position at that time would undertake the 'grand tour' and he was no exception. Although the wealthy of many nations, including America, would undertake similar trips, the 'grand tour' was seen as predominantly English. It was an opportunity for the young English gentleman (and later woman) to experience the art, architecture and culture of what was considered to be the cradle of modern civilisation. The tour would mainly take in France and Italy, and could last anything from a few months to a number of years. Although the tour had its critics, it was considered to be an ideal way of finishing the education of those who would very likely later hold positions of power and influence. The more affluent of those undertaking the tour used it as an opportunity to bring back many works of art, books and pieces of sculpture by the crate load. It was also an opportunity for young men to have more salacious experiences abroad. However, rather than spend his time in the pursuits in which his contemporaries indulged, Sir George passed his in studies which were of a more semi-scientific nature. His work on aeronautics was undertaken with the care and precision expected from a trained scientist; however, he was always to remain humble with regards to his work.

Sir George was quick to point out that flight by attaching wings to a man was a physical impossibility due to a lack of the muscular strength of the pectoral muscles. These muscles accounted for two-thirds of a bird's strength, whereas in a human they could not possibly exceed one-tenth. Therefore, the myth of Icarus would, sadly, always remain a myth.

His magnum opus, a book entitled *Aerial Navigation*, was first published in 1810 and the three-part treatise was soon to be regarded as a classic. Although the main thrust of his work was towards aviation, Sir George also worked on a number of other engineering projects and developed a number of other items, including seatbelts, a self-righting lifeboat, tension-spoke wheels, automatic railway signals and a prototype for an internal combustion engine.

As well as his scientific interests, Sir George was also the MP for Scarborough between 1832 and 1835. For many years he was chairman of the Royal Polytechnic Institution (now known as the University of Westminster), which he helped to found. He died on 15 December 1857, but his name lives on as the Father of British Aeronautics.

COASTLINE

North Yorkshire's coastline begins at Staithes in the north and finishes just short of Flamborough Head. It displays a vast array of different coastal landform types, which include high cliffs, bays, beaches, headlands, stacks and sea caves, all of which have made it popular with smugglers evading the vigilant custom and excise men. This coastline also has some of the finest Jurassic and Cretaceous sections in Britain, and has long been popular with fossil collectors.

STAITHES

Staithes was once one of the largest fishing centres in England, but today the industry has all but disappeared. The village is renowned for its sheltered natural harbour, which is protected by high cliffs and two long breakwaters, and was ideal for the fishermen and their boats. At its height, there were about 300 men engaged in fishing and three times a week a train would run from the station in Staithes taking the catch to the rest of Britain.

The most common boats used were the locally built cobles (pronounced 'cobbles' in Yorkshire, whereas along the Northumbrian coast they are pronounced 'co-bels'). They are ruggedly constructed vessels which are able to withstand the rigours of being launched and landed directly on to the beach. There was also a larger version of this boat, known as a 'Five-Man', which would be manned by seven men: the name actually refers to the fact that its ownership was shared by five people.

The coble is unique to the north-east coast; there is a Scottish coble, but that is a distinctly different vessel. Originally, it was designed to be rowed with long, thin-bladed oars and it would also have a dipping lug sail. Today examples of this craft may also have a small motor. Some people refer to it as the Yorkshire coble, but strictly speaking this is incorrect, as the vessel is also built along the Northumbrian coast. Some experts maintain that they are able to distinguish the difference between them at a glance. The boats are clinker-built, which means that the hull is constructed first and then the internal frame is added later.

It was the introduction of steam trawlers which spelled the end of the fishing industry in Staithes, as its harbour was unable to accommodate these larger vessels. Today few boats remain here and those that do are used to tend lobster pots and to take tourists out on day trips.

A street in Staithes.

In 1745 James Cook came to Staithes as a young man. He began an apprenticeship with a local grocer, but was to leave 12 months later to follow his passion for the sea. It is said that it was during his time at Staithes that he developed this love affair.

In the late 19th century the village attracted a number of artists, who became known as the Staithes Group (also referred to as the Northern Impressionists). It was the painter William Gilbert Foster (1855–1906) who was to make Staithes a popular location for artists, and although he was never actually a member of the group, he was instrumental in encouraging them in their work. Walking through the atmospheric streets of this delightful fishing village, it is not difficult to appreciate the attraction this place had for these artists.

THE MINERALS OF STAITHES

Since time immemorial Staithes has been a centre for mineral extraction and a number of important minerals can be readily found in the area. It is not known whether early man was first attracted here because of its rich source of fishing, or the large quantities of ironstone, which were found to be deposited here; or even the deposits of jet (lignite), which could be easily carved into ornaments and jewellery: artefacts made from this hard form of coal have been unearthed which date back to the Bronze Age. Perhaps we shall never know, but there can be no doubt that this region would have been extremely important to these early inhabitants. Evidence of Iron Age activity has been discovered near Staithes at Roxby Beck.

Another mineral which is found in abundance in the area is potash, and it is mined at Boulby, just a few miles away from the town. Boulby is thought to be the deepest mine in Europe and some of the mining takes place nearly two kilometres beneath the surface. Its main uses are for fertilisers, livestock feed supplements and in a number of industrial processes. Originally, the word 'potash', which is derived from the Dutch word 'potasch', referred to wood ash, from which potassium carbonate was extracted. Today, however, it refers to any potassium compound, of which the most common is potassium chloride. The potash is derived from the minerals which were in the ancient seas and were deposited when they dried up millions of years ago.

RUNSWICK BAY

Evidence shows that Runswick Bay has been inhabited since at least the Bronze Age and there are a number of early burial mounds located near to the village. Its sheltered anchorage meant that it was an ideal place for fishermen and whalers, and, of course, because of its isolated location, it was popular with smugglers. The village is a warren of tiny back streets, making it an ideal place for their nefarious activities.

Life at Runswick Bay can be precarious, as a landslide in 1682 will attest: the whole village, with the exception of one cottage, slipped into the sea. Unbelievably there were no casualties

Runswick Bay.

and the whole community escaped unscathed. Fortunately, two mourners at a wake, realising what was happening, had quickly alerted the village to the danger. Everyone was safely evacuated, and through their speedy actions a human tragedy was averted. After the disaster, the villagers simply rebuilt their homes on the cliff side. In 1858 there was another landslide; however, this time the damage was minimal and only the local iron-smelting works was destroyed. Even as late as 1969 signs that the land was moving were evident as cracks appeared in the walls of the cottages. Since then, however, a sea wall has been constructed, which guarantees the safety of Runswick Bay and its occupants.

In 1901 fishermen from the village were caught in a freak squall and, with no one left to save them from impending doom, it was left to the brave women of Runswick Bay to come to the assistance of their menfolk. These hardy women took the lifeboat and pulled off an impressive rescue.

KETTLENESS

This quiet hamlet was once a busy place, so much so that it warranted its own railway station, which was located on the now dismantled coastal railway. The railway was opened on 3 December 1883 and closed on 5 May 1958.

Kettleness was the site of a Roman signal station. As well as a number of other sites along the coast, Kettleness was important for alum and still bears the scars of this former mining activity. It was an important industry and brought great wealth to the area from about 1604 until 1871. With the exception of one mine in Lancashire, the region was to produce all the English alum supply. Alum was the name given to the specific chemical compound hydrated aluminium potassium sulphate, which has a number of industrial uses. Its value had been known for centuries; the Roman writer and naturalist Pliny the Elder (Gaius Plinius Secundus) described it in his *Naturalis Historia*. This work could

The coast at Kettleness.

possibly be described as his magnum opus and filled 37 books, and was only completed two years before his death. Pliny died during the eruption of Mount Vesuvius on 25 August AD79, which destroyed the cities of Pompeii and Herculaneum.

The coast has always been a dangerous place for the unwary mariner and many have come to grief on the treacherous Kettleness Point. Those who have fallen victim to this capricious stretch of coast include the *Viola* on 19 September 1903, the *Vanland* on 12 August 1911 and the *Golden Sceptre* on 16 January 1912.

WHITBY ABBEY

In 655 the Northumbrian King Oswy won a great victory at the Battle of the River Winwaed (thought to be near to Leeds) in which the tyrant King Penda of Mercia was slain. To fulfil a vow the Northumbrian king gave his daughter Aelffled (who at that time was barely 12 months old) into the service of God. He also gave various plots of land to the church. Two years after the battle, St Hilda, the Abbess of Hartlepool, was to found an abbey at Whitby

(Streoneshalh). The king's daughter was to become the abbey's first novice, and later she would become the abbess. It is said that when St Hilda was the abbess at Whitby the area was overrun with serpents. Through her prayers this pestilence was removed, and the serpents were decapitated and their curled up bodies were turned to stone. Today, we can still find these petrified serpents, but now we know them as fossilised ammonites.

St Hilda was born in 614. Her father was Hereric, who was nephew to King Edwin of Northumbria, and her mother was called Breguswith. Her elder sister was called Herewith, and was married to Æthelric, the brother of King Anna of East Anglia. After becoming widowed, Herewith would later become a nun at an abbey near Paris. Nothing is known about St Hilda's early life, but it is thought that when King Edwin was killed in battle in 633 she travelled to East Anglia to join her sister at court. The Venerable Bede takes up the story as she plans the journey to join her now widowed sister at an abbey. However, before she sets sail, she is recalled by Bishop Aidan, who grants her some land on the

Whitby Abbey.

north bank of the River Wear, where she stays with some companions for a year, observing the monastic rule. Bede clearly refers to the existence of an abbey by the river, but no remains have ever been discovered, except what appears to be a monastic cemetery near to a church called St Hilda's, which could point to its former existence.

Afterwards, she was made abbess of a monastery at Hartlepool. It is said that she was the first woman in the Northumbrian province to have taken her vows. From the abbey at Hartlepool it appears that she travelled to a place called Kaelcacaestir (thought to be Tadcaster) and settled there for some time.

In 657 she founded the abbey at Whitby, where she would remain until her death. Bede describes her as a woman of great energy and a gifted teacher, whose reputation for wisdom drew kings and princes from far and wide asking her advice. She remained a humble and devout Christian throughout her life, and was greatly concerned for the wellbeing of the ordinary folk. He tells us that after devoting her life to the service of Christ she passed away at the age of 66 on 17 November 680 to receive her eternal reward in heaven.

In his *Ecclesiastical History of the English People* the Venerable Bede described how the abbey was the scene of the Synod of Whitby in 664, where the controversy over Easter was finally settled and King Oswy ruled that the Northumbrian Church would use the Roman calculation for its date. Previously, they had been using the Irish calculation for Easter, which was out of step with the rest of the Christian world. It was also ruled that they would adopt the monastic tonsure, again bringing them in line with the rest of Christendom.

Whitby Abbey was a Benedictine monastery for both monks and nuns. The abbey was abandoned in 867 when it was attacked by Vikings during an invasion of Northumbria and York by Ivar the Boneless and his brother,

Halfdan. They were after vengeance following the death of their father, Ragnar Lodbrok, who had been killed by Aella, the king of Northumbria. The abbey was to remain deserted for the next 200 years. William of Malmesbury, a 12th-century historian, wrote that the sacred relics of Whitby Abbey were removed by King Edmund I in 944, when he took control of York. These relics, apparently, ended up in Glastonbury Abbey.

After the Norman Conquest, William rewarded many of his chief men with land. One of his followers who benefitted from this redistribution of land was William 'Algernon' de Percy (born *c.*1040, died 1096). In 1070 he rebuilt York Castle after it was destroyed by the Danes and two years later he took part in William the Conqueror's expedition to Scotland. He died while on the First Crusade in 1096 and was buried at Mount Joy near Jerusalem. His heart, however, was brought home to England by a knight called Ralph Eversly, as it had been de Percy's dying wish to have his heart buried at Whitby Abbey. Obviously the abbey was a special place for William de Percy, and indeed he played a crucial role in the history of this magnificent place: it was he who in 1078 ordered that Whitby Abbey should be re-established and he gave the task of rebuilding it to a soldier monk named Regenfrith (Reinfrid). The new abbey was dedicated to St Peter and St Hilda.

The end came in 1540 with the Dissolution of the Monasteries, and gradually the building fell into ruin and much of its stone was plundered. Though this great building is now only a shell, it is still a stupendous monument, which has the power to delight and impress the many visitors who come to Whitby each year. Standing majestically high upon the cliffs and overlooking Whitby, the awesome ruins of this fabulous abbey will remain a familiar landmark, as it has been for centuries. It is not difficult to imagine that it must have been a welcoming sight for many a sailor returning from his voyage.

CÆDMON

Cædmon is reputed to be the first English religious poet. Very little is known about his life, other than what we have been told by the Venerable Bede: Cædmon lived in the seventh century and was a monk at Whitby Abbey. Bede tells us that he had followed a secular occupation for most of his life, and that part of his duties included looking after the livestock. It appears that he did not develop his talent for poetry until late in life, and that he would leave a feast before being called upon to entertain the other guests. That is, however, until one certain occasion after he had left the table and headed home. After tending to the animals, he settled down to sleep and experienced a strange dream, where a man appeared to him, calling his name. The man asked Cædmon to sing him a song, which he refused to do, saying that he could not sing. He went on to say that was the reason that he left the feast early, but the man was insistent. Eventually, Cædmon began to sing about God the Creator.

The Ruthwell Cross.

The next day he went to see the reeve (his superior), who took him before St Hilda, where he repeated the verses that he had sung in his dream. It was agreed that he had received a gift from God. The abbess told Cædmon a story from the gospel, which he turned into verse and sang to her the next day. The abbess instructed him to give up his secular life and to join the monastic community. Bede states that from that point on the poet turned the gospels into beautiful verses, all composed in Anglo-Saxon, and with which he was able to take the stories of the Bible to the common people.

In the grounds of St Mary's at Whitby stands a replica of the Ruthwell Cross. The original cross dated from the seventh century and had stood at Ruthwell, Dumfriesshire. It is surprising that the original cross has survived over the centuries, as it has suffered a number of misfortunes. The Puritans smashed it and defaced its figures as it was considered an 'idolatrous monument'. In 1802, however, the Reverend Duncan decided to save this ancient monument and rebuilt it. In 1867 Stephens, an Anglo-Saxon scholar, visited the old cross and deciphered some of the runes that were carved on it: 'Cædmon made me'. A number of other scholars agreed with this; but 20 years later the cross had been so worn by the weather that the runic letters were indecipherable, leading many to doubt the veracity of Stephens's claim. The replica at Whitby was placed there in 1892 by Canon Rawnsley, who was one of the founders of the National Trust.

WHITBY

Originally called Streanaeshalh, the coastal town of Whitby has been known by a number of names, including Presteby, Hwytby and Whiteby. The settlement was first founded in 657, at the same time as the abbey was founded. For much of its early history, it was no more than a small fishing port and even by 1540 Whitby had a population of only about 200. It

Along the pier at Whitby.

was the discovery of alum to be mined in the latter part of the reign of Queen Elizabeth I that brought a vast improvement in the port's prosperity. It was the English naturalist, Sir Thomas Chaloner (1559–1615), who was to make this possible. During a trip to Italy he visited some alum works, where he discovered that the local rock used to produce alum was identical to samples which could be found in his native North Yorkshire. This was an important discovery, for alum was of tremendous value as it was used in curing leather, medicines and the fixing of dyes in cloth. At that time the Vatican had held the monopoly on the production and supply of alum, but soon a thriving alum industry developed in North Yorkshire, which brought prosperity to the region. The Vatican authorities, however, were none too pleased and it appears that they excommunicated Sir Thomas.

As a consequence of this new trade Whitby was to prosper and it became a crucial link for

Overlooking the harbour from the famous steps which lead to the abbey and St Mary's Church.

The Grand Turk: *a replica of an 18th-century man-of-war.*

The whalebone arch was erected in 1963 using the jawbone of a blue whale, which is the world's largest animal. The bones were obtained by Thor Dhal of Norway and Graham Leach of Whitby, and the monument is a tribute to the brave men who sailed from Whitby to the cruel seas around the Arctic.

both importing coal for the alum works and exporting the alum. The shipbuilding industry, taking advantage of this trade and a good supply of locally felled oak, was soon to flourish. With the increase in shipping, it became obvious that the piers, which were constructed from wood, were woefully

inadequate and were in dire need of improvement; therefore, in 1632 work began on building stone piers. This was possible through the efforts of Sir Hugh Cholmeley and one of his relations, the Earl of Strafford, who through their influence were able to raise almost £500 in donations. Over time, the piers have been further extended to accommodate a further increase in shipping, and money collected as a duty levied on goods passing through the port paid for this work. In 1702 work began on the east pier, which was to extend 645 feet into the sea.

In 1753 the first of many whaling ships was to set sail from Whitby: its destination was Greenland. By the end of the century the town had become a major centre for the whaling industry. This was to increase the town's fortunes even further, and at its peak there were 55 whaling ships based at Whitby. Between 1753 and 1833 about 2,760 whales and over 25,000 seals were brought back to the port, where the blubber was made into oil in great boiler houses. Very little of the whale was wasted, as the skin would be used for leather, the cartilage

The Grand Turk's *figurehead.*

The church of St Mary's in Whitby.

Far right: The private entrance to the Cholmeley family pew.

Right: In a niche beside the private entrance is a memorial to Francis Huntrodd and his wife Mary, who were both born on the same day in 1600; they were married on their birthday and died within five hours of each other on their 80th birthday.

for glue, and the oil from the blubber would be used for soap, margarine, paints, candles, lubricants and even as a fuel for street lighting. The industry finally fell into decline after the discovery of petrol oils and other lubricants.

Another industry which was to make Whitby famous was the production of jewellery from locally mined jet. Formed from the fossilised remains of decaying wood, jet had been mined in the area since the Bronze Age. It was popular with the Romans, who were to mine it extensively. However, it was to reach its peak of

popularity in the mid-19th century after Queen Victoria began to wear it as mourning jewellery after the death of Prince Albert.

In 1839 George Hudson completed his railway network, which connected Whitby to York and helped to open the town to tourism. This was yet another stage in the development of the town's fortunes. Although the town is perhaps better known today as the destination for the tourist trade, it possesses a modern port, which is capable of handling a wide range of cargoes. It is ideally located for shipping to and from Europe, especially the Scandinavian countries.

THE STORY OF DRACULA

In 1897 Abraham Stoker (better known as 'Bram') published his famous novel *Dracula*, which is partly set in Whitby. Born in Dublin in 1847, Stoker was a sickly child and had been bedridden until the age of seven, at which age he made a full recovery and started school. It was this prolonged period of illness which he claimed had proved beneficial to him in his later life, as it had given him the opportunity to develop his imagination. Fully recovered from his poor health, he grew up into a fine young man and even gained a reputation as an athlete while at university. As well as his sporting prowess, he would become a respected theatre critic for a Dublin newspaper while still a student.

It was through a favourable review, which he had written about Sir Henry Irving's performance as Hamlet, that he was first brought to the attention of the great actor. Sir Henry invited the young critic to dine with him at his hotel, and they became firm friends. Later Stoker would become his personal assistant, and for a time he was employed as a civil servant.

In 1878 he married Florence Balcombe, a celebrated beauty who had previously had Oscar Wilde as one of her suitors. Soon after their marriage they moved to London, where he would eventually become the business manager of the Lyceum Theatre. To supplement his income, he wrote novels, and after spending a number of years researching stories about vampires and European folklore, he wrote *Dracula*. Strangely, although his work with Sir Henry would take him around the world, he would never visit Eastern Europe, even though it would feature heavily in his famous novel.

It was during a holiday in Whitby in 1890 that Stoker would find the inspiration for his book, and he even discovered the name *Dracula* in a public library. He incorporated much local folklore into his story, including the grounding

A 12-pound gun which was rescued from the wreck of the African Transport off the coast at Kettleness.

This is a monument to William Scoresby, the inventor of the crow's nest, who was born on 3 May 1760 in the village of Cropton. He was taken out of school at the age of nine to become a farmer, but due to the cruel treatment he received he left to go to sea. He became a successful captain and whaler.

Sandsend: located a few miles along the coast from Whitby.

of a Russian ship called *Dmitri*, which he called *Demeter* in his book. The novel was written in an epistolary style, in the form of the journal of Jonathan Harker.

Bram Stoker died on 20 April 1912 in London, and his ashes now rest, mingled with those of his son, in the Golders Green Crematorium in London.

ROBIN HOOD'S BAY

Legend has it that Robin Hood's Bay was originally founded by the famous outlaw from Sherwood Forest. We must, however, disregard this as a romantic tale for, in truth, the village would have been established long before this folk hero wandered through the land, robbing from the rich and giving to the poor.

When humans first occupied the area, around 10,000 years ago, the land would have been far different from today. At that time there would have been no sea separating the Continent from the British Isles, but a continuous land mass that was covered with a

This tunnel was once used by smugglers to hide their contraband.

dense coniferous forest, which stretched from the Pennines to the Urals. In about 4000BC the oceans began to rise, thereby creating the British Isles. This, however, would not be the first time that the land would have been submerged, as millions of years before this the whole of the area would have lain under an ocean. Robin Hood's Bay and the surrounding area are rich in fossils, bearing out this fact.

Around the district can be found a wealth of evidence of these early human inhabitants, for they have left a number of barrows and tumuli. Many artefacts have also been unearthed, such as sepulchral vases, flint axes and knives. It is not known whether Robin Hood's Bay would have been a settlement at this time, but it is clear that there would have been some form of human activity in close proximity. By the fourth century AD, however, there is evidence that the Romans had built a fort at Ravenscar. In 1771 a stone was discovered by builders, which bore the inscription: 'Justinian, governor of the province, and Vindicianus, prefect of soldiers, built this fort' (now in Whitby Museum).

Robin Hood's Bay.

This board lists the vessels which the Robin Hood's Bay lifeboat has rescued.

The village was not known as Robin Hood's Bay until the 16th century (even today it is known by the locals as 'Baytown' or simply 'the Bay'). Where it got its name from remains a mystery; however, as with all mysteries, there are a number of suggestions, with some more plausible than others. One of the most popular theories is actually based on historical fact. In the 12th century the king of Norway entered Whitby with a number of ships and robbed the abbey, and it was from this incident that the story was to grow. It was said that the abbot, a man named Richard, asked Robin Hood for help against these invaders, and in return he promised him a royal pardon. As the pirates scaled the cliffs towards the abbey, Robin and his men hurled boulders and fired arrows down upon them, killing about 70 of the invaders.

Another, and perhaps more plausible theory, concerns the barrows, which can be found on the nearby moors; as the famous local priest and scholar Canon John Christopher Atkinson was to point out in 1891. He believed that the name was

derived from folk etymology: Robin Hood being the name of an ancient forest spirit or elf and sometimes known as Robin Goodfellow or Puck. Atkinson went on to say that it was highly

A street in Robin Hood's Bay.

probable that local folk thought that this ancient spirit haunted the barrows and would name them Robin Hood's Butts. Over time, the association was changed from the spirit and simply transferred to the outlaw. This would have been further reinforced as the barrows resembled the mounds of butts used behind archery targets. These two theories are among the many circulating as to how the village derived its name. It is highly unlikely that we will ever know the answer, but it would be nice to imagine this colourful 'folk hero' and his merry men fighting off pirates from across the North Sea and perhaps practising their archery among the barrows.

As for many of its neighbours along the north-east coast, the 18th century was a turbulent time for Robin Hood's Bay. Smuggling was rife and it was not uncommon to see running battles off the shoreline between the smugglers and the customs and excise men. Although hazardous, smuggling was a lucrative trade in which vast fortunes could be made. Indeed, such great profits were achievable that often whole communities were involved, even sometimes including the local squire. Heavily taxed commodities such as tobacco, spirits and tea were available on the Continent at a fraction of the price, and demand for these goods was high. Few, if any, would see anything wrong in using this contraband. Many, in fact, would have been highly offended if it had been suggested that by purchasing smuggled goods they were complicit in a crime.

The seas were vast and using fast ships, mainly under the cover of night, the risk of detection or capture was minimal. However, losses to the revenue in unpaid duties became such a serious problem that the government was forced to take stronger measures. Vessels on both sides became larger and more heavily armed and the times became more violent. Although anti-smuggling laws were tightened, if caught, a smuggler might not necessarily expect to end his days on the end of a rope; many were simply deported, while others found themselves pressed into either army or navy service. Ironically, those who found themselves in the navy often progressed rapidly through the ranks; this fact, not surprisingly, often caused much resentment among the other ratings. Their speedy promotion was often due to the high quality of their seamanship skills, which they had acquired while avoiding detection by the revenue cutters.

At the height of the smuggling activities, Robin Hood's Bay was notorious and possibly the source of the biggest thorn in the side of the excisemen of the north-west coast. As the 19th century progressed, there appears to have been a decline in smuggling and today it is hard to believe that this picturesque village had such a violent and dramatic past. It must be remembered, however, that the village obtained its main source of income through more legitimate activities and once possessed a large fishing community.

Robin Hood's Bay was the childhood home of the writer Leo Walmsley (1892–1966). Born in Shipley, Bradford, his family moved to the Bay when he was two. He was to grow up with a deep love of the coast and surrounding moorland, which would materialise in his books, especially his *Bramblewick* trilogy, written during the 1930s and set in Robin Hood's Bay. During World War One he served with the Royal Flying Corps as an observer and was awarded the Military Cross. After being sent home after an aeroplane crash, he pursued a career in writing and many of his works were autobiographical. A prolific writer, who will probably be best remembered for his books based in Robin Hood's Bay, he died on 8 June 1966 in Fowey, Cornwall.

RAVENSCAR AND MAD KING GEORGE

It is rumoured that during one of George III's spells of madness he was brought to Ravenscar by Dr Francis Willis. The doctor had reputedly brought the king here to avoid publicity and he

Scarborough's coat of arms.

incarcerated the monarch in his house, which at the time was called Peak Hall. It is now a hotel called Raven Hall.

George III was the second longest reigning British monarch after Queen Victoria, and was on the throne for 60 years. He was a popular king, and one of the main causes of this popularity was his interest in farming and agriculture, which was seen by a few as not being a subject suitable for a monarch, but it was one which endeared him to his subjects. The king had his first attack of what was thought to be insanity in 1788. Recent research has revealed that he may never have been insane, but was in fact suffering from a rare disorder called porphyria. Its name is derived from Greek and means 'purple pigment', which is a reference to the purple discolouration of faeces and urine experienced by a patient during an attack. The disorder primarily affects the nervous system, which can result in hallucinations, depression and anxiety. It was first explained by Dr Felix Hoppe-Seyler, the German physiologist and chemist, in 1874.

By 1810 George III was virtually blind through cataracts and during the last 10 years of his life his health would rapidly deteriorate. As well as being increasingly deaf, he would completely lose his sight. Increasingly isolated, he would never learn of his wife's death in 1818. During the final weeks of his life, as well as being unable to walk, he once spoke nonsense continuously for 58 hours. He died on 29 January 1820.

It is highly debatable whether the king actually ever did visit Ravenscar or stay at Peak Hall, and in all probability it is just a good story. The house, which was built for Captain William Childs in 1774, did not come into the possession of the Willis family until the early 1830s, by which time the king had been dead for over 10 years.

SCARBOROUGH

Considered to be Britain's first seaside resort, Scarborough has been delighting the holidaymaker for well over 300 years. The town

first became popular after the discovery of its spring waters and their medicinal properties. It has been documented that bathing machines were first used in the town in 1735 and only a year later an engraving produced by John Setterington shows bathers using them.

According to a mediaeval Icelandic saga, Scarborough got its name from two Viking brothers, who had sailed the coast of Britain and Ireland in search of plunder and adventure. Their names were Kormak and Thorgils (also known by his nickname of Skardi, due to his harelip). Kormak, although renowned as a poet, was a wild extrovert man with curly locks of raven-black hair, whereas his brother was the silent brooding type. In 966 they established a fort on what is thought to be the ruins of a Roman signal station and called it Skardaborg (after Thorgils's nickname). Kormak was eventually killed during a raid on Scotland. It appears that there are a number of alternative suggestions as to how Scarborough was founded; however, the historian, Sir Frank Stenton (1880–1967), wrote in his acclaimed book *Anglo-Saxon England* that it was the Viking brothers who were the founders of the

said that Kormak also possessed a nickname, which was Fleinn (arrow), and from that we derive the East Yorkshire place name of Flamborough.

The harbour of Scarborough can be traced back as far as 1225, when local men were given 40 oaks by Henry III from his woods so that they could construct a harbour. Twenty-six years later the king was to grant a charter which enabled the townsfolk to build a safer harbour from timber and stone. In 1564 the harbour was rebuilt with money and materials granted by Elizabeth I. In total, they were given £500 in money, 100 tons of timber and 6 tons of iron for the reconstruction. George II was to pass an Act in 1732 which enabled the harbour to be enlarged by building Vincent's Pier and the present East Pier.

A monument celebrating the millennium. It was created as a modern interpretation of a Viking commemorative stone and is a reminder of Scarborough's Viking heritage.

SCARBOROUGH CASTLE

The dramatic ruins which are perched high upon the rocky headland overlooking Scarborough are of a 12th-century castle. Construction of this stronghold was begun by William le Gros in the 1130s. In 1154, however, the castle was seized by Henry II, and it was he who was responsible for the erection of the

town. So perhaps we can conclude that this is the most likely theory. He also quotes (in his footnotes) that E.V. Gordon wrote in his *Introduction to Old Norse* (1957) that it was

Left: Anne Brontë's grave at St Mary's in Scarborough.

Far left: The ancient church of St Mary's in Scarborough received considerable damage during the English Civil War and although the north aisle was subsequently rebuilt, the great quire and north transept remain ruined.

*Scarborough
Castle.*

keep, which can be seen today. Further additions were to be made to this mediaeval castle by King John and Henry III.

Over the centuries, the castle has been the scene of many conflicts. In 1312 it was besieged for two weeks by rebel barons, with the siege only ending when Piers Gaveston, 1st Earl of Cornwall and Edward II's favourite, surrendered to Aymer de Valence, 2nd Earl of Pembroke. Shortly afterwards, Gaveston was murdered by two Welshmen at Blacklow Hill in Warwickshire; he was run through with a sword and then beheaded as he lay dying. Edward II flew into a rage when he heard of Gaveston's death and vowed to avenge his murder. He eventually succeeded 10 years later when he had the Earl of Lancaster killed.

During the English Civil War the castle and town changed hands seven times and eventually Parliament ordered that the keep should be demolished to prevent the Royalists from using it. The castle was again damaged in anger when shots were fired at it as a squadron of German ships opened fire on Scarborough during World War One.

The castle was used as a prison in the 17th and 18th centuries, and later it was used as a military barracks. Today this magnificent ruin is managed by English Heritage and is a familiar sight for all those who have visited this seaside resort.

THE GRAND HOTEL

Reputed to have once been the largest hotel in Europe, the Grand Hotel was specially built to accommodate the growing Victorian trend for the seaside holiday, and specifically to cater for the more affluent clientele. Unquestionably one of Scarborough's iconic buildings, this magnificent edifice has dominated the skyline of the town's south bay since 1867. It was described by Sir Nicholas Pevsner (1902–83), one of the 20th-century's foremost writers on architecture, as 'a High [sic] Victorian gesture of assertion and confidence'. It was designed by the renowned architect Cuthbert Brodrick, who had designed Leeds Town Hall and another iconic Victorian masterpiece, Leeds Corn Exchange. His initial idea was to produce a building that would represent the seasons,

The Grand Hotel

months, weeks and days of the year – four towers, 12 floors, 52 chimneys and 365 rooms.

Scarborough's economy was booming as more and more Victorians flocked to the seaside resort, driven by their passion for a holiday. In the early 1860s, a group of businessmen, seeing a potentially profitable opportunity, formed a syndicate with the sole purpose of taking advantage of the trend. Their idea was to construct a hotel which was of such grandeur and luxury as to attract the most affluent and discerning visitors to their town. First, a site was to be found and one that would command stunning views with which to impress the wealthy guests: this was found at the top of St Nicholas's Cliff. The land already housed a number of properties, and these would require demolishing to make way for the fabulous hotel. One of the buildings which was on the site was called Wood's Lodging. On visits to Scarborough, the Brontë sisters had stayed at this property on many occasions and it was in this building that Anne Brontë died from

tuberculosis at the age of 29. (Her grave can be found at St Mary's Church, in the shadow of Scarborough Castle.)

Initially the new hotel was to be called Cliff Hotel, and work was to commence on its construction in 1863. However, progress

Above the main entrance of the Grand Hotel.

ground to a halt two years later when funds dried up. The project was only half completed and had already cost the syndicate £90,000, but with no more money they were unable to continue and were forced to sell their interests at a loss, eventually recouping just short of half the money that they had spent. The new owners, the Grand Hotel Ltd, took over the project in 1866 and in a little over 12 months the hotel was ready for opening. Its new name was certainly more befitting of its appearance, as it was (and still is) a truly 'grand' structure.

The hotel was officially opened on 24 July 1867 and the occasion was celebrated with a lavish banquet for 200 guests, who had been specially invited from throughout the country. Each guest was presented with a beautifully illuminated copy of the menu as a keepsake. The festivities did not end with the banquet, for the following night they were treated to a fabulous ball, which included a sumptuous buffet supper. The dancing began with a waltz called *Grand Hotel*, which had been specially composed for the occasion.

Standing on the golden sands of South Bay, it is not hard to imagine how our Victorian forefathers would have been spellbound by this splendid building. Time, however, has brought mixed fortunes for this elegant hotel. During the hostilities of World War One it was badly damaged when a squadron of German warships appeared off the shores of Scarborough. At 8am on 16 December 1914 the squadron, which consisted of the battle cruisers *Derfflinger, Von der Tann* and *Kolberg*, commenced their bombardment of Scarborough. The attack was to last 30 minutes, during which about 500 shells were fired. It resulted in the deaths of 17 civilians and a further 80 were wounded. This indiscriminate slaughter of innocent civilians was to irrevocably change the face of warfare forever.

As would be expected from such a heavy bombardment, there was much damage done to a number of properties in the town, including the hotel, which received two hits, resulting in £10,000-worth of damage. Fortunately, there appear to have been no casualties, although a waiter had a close shave when a room that he had only just vacated was destroyed. There is an amusing story often told about this episode. It may be apocryphal, but it is worth retelling: the waiter was a poor timekeeper and had on many occasions been warned about his punctuality. This time he had just received his final warning when the bombardment started. After his near miss, he was never late again. Although the Germans had momentarily succeeded in implying that the Royal Navy no longer ruled the waves with their impudent attack, it was a hollow victory, for the killing of innocent civilians outraged public opinion, and for the rest of the war 'Remember Scarborough' became a recruiting slogan. Even if it succeeded in striking terror into the hearts of the English people, this was short-lived, but the outrage and indignation felt by the country at large would live on.

Another German squadron, which attacked Hartlepool on the same day, was not so lucky and was beaten off by a territorial coastal battery. Although the battery was completely outgunned by the Germans, it fought bravely and fiercely, inflicting heavy casualties on the German raiders. A month later, the Germans attempted another raid, this time on the British fishing fleet, but the Royal Navy were ready for them and they were badly mauled. The Royal Navy sent a clear message to the world, and that was that Britannia still ruled the waves.

During World War Two the hotel was commandeered by the RAF to billet its trainees. Anti-aircraft machine guns were positioned in the hotel's cupolas, but were never to be fired in anger. Today, a plaque can be seen next to the main entrance, commemorating those days when the grand old building was drafted into military service. Over the years, the building has had its fair share of detractors and some maintain that it is an ugly Victorian monstrosity, which should be torn down. But it would be a sad day if this minority were to get their way, for we would surely be the poorer for its loss. The Grand Hotel is an exquisite example of Victorian architecture at its best and a landmark of which Scarborough should be rightly proud.

SCARBOROUGH FAIR

Are you going to Scarborough Fair?
Parsley, sage, rosemary, and thyme.

Many will remember this being sung by Simon and Garfunkel in the 1960s, but the actual song dates back centuries to the Elizabethan period and is a traditional English 'riddle' song. The origins of the song are unknown, but the melody is undoubtedly much older than 16th century. Although many of its lyrics are shrouded in mystery, with its impossible tasks set by a man to a former lover, the Scarborough Fair of its title once existed.

In 1253 Scarborough received a royal charter that allowed the town to hold an annual fair, which attracted traders from all over Europe. It ran for six weeks from Assumption Day (15 August) until Michaelmas Day (29 September). The fair was eventually abandoned in the 18th century.

THE ROTUNDA MUSEUM

At four o'clock on Monday 31 August 1829 62 gentlemen sat down to a lavish dinner at Hanson's Hotel. They had paid the princely sum of 13 shillings and sixpence each for the privilege. The occasion was the opening of the Scarborough Museum. Flags were hoisted from the windows of the museum and half a brick was presented to Edward Venables-Vernon-Harcourt, the current Archbishop of York.

The museum was designed to the specifications of William Smith (1769–1839), who lived in Scarborough between 1824 and 1826. He was known as the Father of English Geology, although he would not receive instant recognition for his work. In fact, his work was overlooked by the scientific community at first,

The stunning Rotunda Museum.

A cupola on top of the spa.

and due to his humble beginnings, he found it difficult to mix readily with the upper echelons of learned society. After a spell in a debtors' prison, he returned home to find a bailiff waiting for him. Left without a home, he would spend the next few years as an itinerant surveyor. Sir John Johnstone, who was one of his employers, recognised his talent and eventually made sure that he received the acknowledgement that he deserved.

The museum was described in Branwell Brontë's unfinished novel, and there can be no doubt that his sister, Anne, would have visited it, though she would not have known the distinctive rectangular side wings, for these were not added until the 1860s.

THE SPA

In the 1620s the healing natural mineral waters of Scarborough were discovered by the wife of one of the town's leading citizens, Mrs Thomasin Farrer. She soon told all her friends and neighbours about the medicinal qualities of the spring water. Word of this spread like

The ornamental outlet for Scarborough's mineral water. However, the water here is no longer fit for human consumption.

wildfire, and before long Scarborough was the destination of thousands seeking miraculous cures from taking the waters.

By the 1690s, the town had not only become famous for its spa, but had also become the first English seaside resort, and by the mid-18th century regular horse races took place on the beach.

In the early 18th century a basic wooden structure was erected for the dispensing of the waters. It was called the 'Spaw' House (this being the original spelling of spa, which was used until the early 19th century).

In 1827 the Cliff Bridge was opened to give better access to the spa. In 1839 the impressive 'Gothic Saloon', which included a 500-seat concert hall, was opened, having been designed by Henry Wyatt. But as soon as it was opened it was discovered that it was too small to cater for the number of visitors who were coming to Scarborough. Something had to be done, so Sir Joseph Paxton was commissioned to redesign the spa. Sir Joseph was a landscape designer and architect with impeccable credentials and he had been responsible for creating the grounds

of Chatsworth as head gardener and subsequently designing the Crystal Palace. In 1858 his stunning new spa was opened, but, sadly, on 8 September 1876 it was destroyed by fire. Ironically, all that remained standing was the building which he had been invited to replace.

With no time to lose, another building was constructed and in June 1879 the new Grand Hall was opened. This building still stands, delighting visitors to this day. The spring water can no longer be taken, as it was discovered in the 1930s that it was no longer fit for human consumption. But the elegance of former times can still be experienced at the spa in the Grand Hall, the Spa Theatre or even listening to one of the open-air concerts in the Suncourt.

The Cliff Bridge was first opened on 19 July 1827 to much pomp and ceremony. The occasion drew large crowds and a mail coach was driven across it at speed, with a sailor balancing precariously on top.

AFTERWORD

The county of North Yorkshire is wonderfully diverse and any writer can only hope at best to scratch the surface of its rich history, as to comprehensively present the full story of this region would fill many volumes. I hope, however, that this book has encouraged the reader to delve deeper into what this county has to offer and that you have enjoyed our brief journey as much as I have.

BIBLIOGRAPHY

Bede. (1990). *Ecclesiastical History of the English People*. London: Penguin Books.

Churchill, W.S. (2002). *A History of the English-Speaking Peoples (The Birth of Britain)*. London: Cassell.

Crofton, I. and Ayton, J. (2005). *Brewer's Britain and Ireland*. London: Weidenfeld and Nicolson.

Fraser, A. (1969). *Mary, Queen of Scots*. London: Phoenix Press.

Gilbert, M. (2000). *Churchill – A Life*. London: Pimlico.

Johnson, D. (1996). *Discovery – Walks in the Yorkshire Dales – The Northern Dales*. Wilmslow, Cheshire: Sigma Leisure.

Johnson, D. (1996). *Discovery – Walks in the Yorkshire Dales – The Southern Dales*. Wilmslow, Cheshire: Sigma Leisure.

Marshall, A. (2004). *Oliver Cromwell – Soldier – The Military Life of a Revolutionary at War*. London: Brassey's.

Nuttgens, P. (2007). *The History of York*. Pickering: Blackthorn Press.

Pevsner, N. (2002). *Yorkshire – The North Riding*. New Haven: Yale University Press.

Pevsner, N. (2003). *Yorkshire: The West Riding*. New Haven: Yale University Press.

Stenton, F. (1971). *Anglo-Saxon England*. Oxford: Oxford University Press.